P9-DEO-884

50 Literacy Strategies

Step by Step

Second Edition

GAIL E. TOMPKINS
California State University, Fresno

PEARSON

Merrill
Prentice Hall

Upper Saddle River, New Jersey
Columbus, Ohio

Library of Congress Cataloging-in-Publication Data

Tompkins, Gail E.
   50 literacy strategies: step by step / Gail E. Tompkins.—2nd ed.
     p. cm.
   Includes bibliographical references.
   ISBN 0-13-112188-X
   1. Language arts (Elementary)—United States. 2. Language arts (Middle
school)—United States. I. Title: Fifty literacy strategies. II. Title.

LB1576 .T653 2004
372.6'044—dc21

2002035685

Vice President and Publisher: Jeffery W. Johnston
Editor: Linda Ashe Montgomery
Development Editor: Hope Madden
Production Editor: Mary M. Irvin
Design Coordinator: Diane C. Lorenzo
Text Design and Production Coordination: Carlisle Publishers Services
Cover Designer: Linda Sorrells-Smith
Cover Art: SuperStock
Production Manager: Pamela D. Bennett
Director of Marketing: Ann Castel Davis
Marketing Manager: Darcy Betts Prybella
Marketing Coordinator: Tyra Poole

This book was set in Optima by Carlisle Communications, Ltd., and was printed and bound by Courier
Kendallville, Inc. The cover was printed by Phoenix Color Corp.

Pearson Prentice Hall™ is a trademark of Pearson Education, Inc.
Pearson® is a registered trademark of Pearson plc
Prentice Hall® is a registered trademark of Pearson Education, Inc.
Merrill® is a registered trademark of Pearson Education, Inc.

Pearson Education Ltd.
Pearson Education Singapore Pte. Ltd.
Pearson Education Canada, Ltd.
Pearson Education—Japan

Pearson Education Australia Pty. Limited.
Pearson Education North Asia Ltd.
Pearson Educacion de Mexico, S.A. de C.V.
Pearson Education Malaysia Pte. Ltd.

10 9 8 7 6 5 4
ISBN 0-13-112188-X

Preface

Do you need an effective alternative to traditional reading workbook and seatwork activities?

Do you want a handy instructional reference with step-by-step guidelines for a student teacher or teaching intern?

Here is a conveniently organized resource for all elementary and middle school teachers. These strategies are research based and classroom tested, and can be used in literature focus units, reading and writing workshop, or thematic units. Many new instructional strategies, such as interactive writing, story retelling, and word sorts, have been recommended for classroom use, but locating information about how to implement these strategies can be difficult and time consuming. Each strategy begins with a grid that recommends the most appropriate usage and answers the following questions at a glance:

1. Does the strategy fit best as part of a literature focus unit, for reading and writing workshop, for literature circles, or for reading and writing during the thematic unit?
2. For what grade level does the strategy work best?
3. Does the strategy work best for individuals, pairs, small groups, or the entire class?

Here is a sample grid to show you how quickly instructional decisions can be made:

● literature focus units	● preK	○ individual
○ literature circles	● K–2	○ pairs
○ reading-writing workshop	● 3–5	○ small group
● thematic units	● 6–8	● whole class

Of course, these are only recommendations. Once you become comfortable with the basic steps, you may want to experiment and augment these ideas with your own.

After the grid, the instructional strategy is described briefly and the benefits of using the strategy are explained. Next, the steps in using that specific literacy strategy are listed. Best of all, applications and examples are provided that describe ways experienced teachers have used the instructional procedure. References allow you to find out more about the strategy on your own and demonstrate that the strategy has been proven successful in helping students develop into capable readers and writers.

KEY FEATURES

- Strategies are arranged alphabetically and numbered for easy reference. Inside the cover of the book is an index that groups the strategies by concept, providing another easy guide to finding the strategy you need.
- Everything you need to know to implement the strategy effectively and quickly is included in a consistent, easy-to-understand format.
- Complete step-by-step instructions with illustrations are provided to guide you.
- Applications and examples are included to demonstrate strategies and to stimulate your own creativity.
- **New!** ELL Notes point out the strategies most effective for English language learners.

USING THIS BOOK

Fifty Literacy Strategies: Step by Step can be used as a supplementary textbook in any reading, literacy, or language arts methods course. It can also be used as a core text for inservice training or staff development workshops. Gail E. Tompkins has written several major textbooks: *Language Arts: Content and Teaching Strategies,* fifth edition; *Literacy for the 21st Century: A Balanced Approach,* third edition; *Teaching Writing: Balancing Process and Product,* fourth edition; and *Literacy for the 21st Century: Teaching Reading and Writing in Pre-Kindergarten through Grade 4,* all published by Merrill/Prentice Hall. This guide was written to complement each of these textbooks and reflects the same balanced approach that is so popular with professors and preservice and inservice teachers across the country.

ACKNOWLEDGMENTS

I want to express my appreciation to my students at California State University, Fresno, and to the Teacher Consultants in the San Joaquin Valley Writing Project for demonstrating literacy strategies for me and sharing student samples with me. In particular, I want to thank these teachers: Eileen Boland, Tenaya Middle School, Fresno, CA; Linda Boroski, John Muir Elementary School, Fresno, CA; Roberta Dillon, Armona Union Elementary School, Armona, CA; Whitney Donnelly, Williams Ranch Elementary School, Penn Valley, CA; Marceen Farsakian, Turner Elementary School, Fresno, CA; Parthy Ford, Whittier Elementary School, Lawton, OK; Laurie Goodman, Pioneer Middle School, Hanford, CA; Mark Mattingly, Central Junior High School, Lawton, OK; Susan McCloskey, Lowell Elementary School, Fresno, CA; Kristi McNeal, Cooper Hills Elementary School, Clovis, CA; Carol Ochs, Monroe Elementary School, Norman, OK; Tamara Oliver and Carol Surabian, Washington Intermediate School, Dinuba, CA; Judy Reeves, Western Hills Elementary School, Lawton, OK; Jenny Reno, Lawton Public Schools, Lawton, OK; Judy Roberts, Madera Unified School District, Madera, CA; Cheryl Schellenberg, Lincoln Elementary School, Dinuba, CA; Terry Scrivener, Millview Elementary School, Madera, CA; Susan Zumwalt, Terry Elementary School, Selma, CA. I also want to thank my colleagues who have shared their expertise with me, most especially Lea McGee, University of Alabama; Adrienne Herrell, California State University, Fresno; and Shirley Carson, East Central Oklahoma University.

Thanks also to the reviewers of my manuscript for their insights and comments: Joyce C. Fine, Florida International University; Wilma Kuhlman, University of Nebraska at Omaha; J. Susan Lynch, University of Central Florida; Cheryl S. Turner, Georgia State University; Gilbert Valadez, Radford University; and Yvonne Tixiery Vigil, University of Nebraska, Omaha.

Finally, I am indebted to Jeff Johnston and his team at Merrill/Prentice Hall in Columbus, Ohio, who produce so many high-quality publications. I am honored to be a Merrill author. I want to express my appreciation to Linda Montgomery, my editor, Hope Madden, my development editor, Mary Irvin, my production editor, and Melissa Gruzs, my copyeditor. Thanks to all of you.

Contents

1 "All About . . . " Books

● literature focus units	○ preK	● individual
○ literature circles	● K–2	● pairs
● reading-writing workshop	○ 3–5	○ small group
● thematic units	○ 6–8	○ whole class

Young children write "All About . . . " books on familiar topics. They put together a booklet with four or five pages, write a word, phrase, or sentence on each page, and add illustrations. Teachers and students read the book together, and teachers help students revise or edit their books before they share from the author's chair. This is the first type of book that young children or other beginning writers make (Bonin, 1988; Sowers, 1985; Tompkins, 2004). The organization of the book is simple, with one characteristic, example, or fact written and illustrated on each page.

STEP BY STEP

The steps in writing an "All About . . . " book are:

1. *Choose a topic for the book.* Students choose a topic that is familiar or interesting to them, or teachers suggest a broad topic related to a thematic unit the class is studying.

2. *Gather and organize ideas for writing.* Students brainstorm possible ideas for what they will write on each page, or draw pictures for each page.

3. *Write the book.* Students write words, phrases, or sentences on each page to accompany pictures they have drawn.

4. *Read the book with the teacher.* Students conference with the teacher, reread their books, and make revising and editing changes as necessary. Students often add more words to what they have written, correct spelling errors, and add necessary punctuation marks. Sometimes teachers or students type final copies of the books on the computer after the conference, but other students "publish" their books without recopying them.

Making an "All About . . . " book with three, four, or five pages is an excellent writing experience for students learning English. Students use an easy-to-learn structure; they write a fact using a sentence or two on each page, and those students who are very artistic embellish their books with detailed illustrations that extend the information presented in the text.

5. *Share the completed book with the class.* As the final step, students sit in the author's chair to read their completed books to classmates. Then classmates clap, offer congratulatory comments, and ask questions.

APPLICATIONS AND EXAMPLES

Students often make "All About . . . " books as part of writing workshop and during thematic units. During writing workshop, students choose their own topics for these books, writing about their families, pets, vacations, hobbies, and other experiences. For example, a first grader wrote this book about "My Precious Cat" during writing workshop:

Page 1:	*My cat is named Meow because she meows and meows all the time.*
Page 2:	*I feed Meow Cat Chow in her dish every morning.*
Page 3:	*Meow got lost once for 6 days but then she came home. She was all dirty but she was safe.*

FIGURE 1–1   Two Pages From a First Grader's "Seeds" Book

Page 4:   *Meow is mostly all black but she has white on her toes. Her fur is very silky.*

Page 5:   *Meow sleeps on my bed and she licks me with her scratchy tongue.*

This student wrote about a familiar topic, and on each page of her book she focused on a different piece of information about her cat.

During thematic units, students write similar books. For example, when students are studying plants, they can write books about plants in general or about one of these topics:

- how plants grow
- different kinds of plants, such as flowers, trees, and vegetables
- parts of a plant
- plants we eat

The topics that students choose to write "All About . . . " books on reflect the teacher's goals for the thematic unit and the information that students are learning. Two pages from a first grader's "Seeds" book are shown in Figure 1–1. This student wrote about information learned during the unit, and he was able to spell most of the words correctly by locating them on a word wall posted in the classroom. The few remaining spelling errors were corrected during a conference with the teacher.

Older students who have not had much writing experience can also write "All About . . . " books as a first report-writing experience. Students can write "All About . . . " books about the Oregon Trail or ancient Greece in social studies, about insects, minerals, or simple machines in science, or about measurement, time, or money in math.

REFERENCES

Bonin, S. (1988). Beyond storyland: Young writers can tell it other ways. In T. Newkirk & N. Atwell (Eds.), *Understanding writing* (2nd ed.) (pp. 47–51). Portsmouth, NH: Heinemann.

Sowers, S. (1985). The story and the "all about" book. In J. Hansen, T. Newkirk, & D. Graves (Eds.), *Breaking ground: Teachers relate reading and writing in the elementary school* (pp. 73–82). Portsmouth, NH: Heinemann.

Tompkins, G. E. (2004). *Teaching writing: Balancing process and product* (4th ed.). Upper Saddle River, NJ: Merrill/Prentice Hall.

2 Alphabet Books

- ● literature focus units
- ○ literature circles
- ○ reading-writing workshop
- ● thematic units

- ○ preK
- ● K–2
- ● 3–5
- ● 6–8

- ○ individual
- ○ pairs
- ○ small group
- ● whole class

Alphabet books are 26 pages in length, with one page featuring each letter. Students construct alphabet books as part of social studies and science themes or on topics related to literature focus units, much like the alphabet trade books published for children, such as *The Icky Bug Alphabet Book* (Pallotta, 1986) and *A Is for Africa* (Onyefulu, 1993). Students usually make alphabet books collaboratively as a class. Small groups of students or individual students can make alphabet books, but with 26 pages to complete, it is an arduous task. Students share what they have learned about the topic through the alphabet book, and these books are added to the classroom library after they are published (Tompkins, 2004).

STEP BY STEP

The steps in constructing a class alphabet book are:

1. *Examine alphabet trade books published for children.* Students can examine the format and design of books such as *Eating the Alphabet: Fruits and Vegetables From A to Z* (Ehlert, 1989), *V Is for Vanishing: An Alphabet of Endangered Animals* (Mullins, 1993), and *Illuminations* (Hunt, 1989), or alphabet books made by students in other classes.

2. *Make an alphabet chart.* Teachers write the letters of the alphabet in a column on a long sheet of butcher paper, leaving space for students to write several words beginning with each letter on the chart. Students brainstorm words for the alphabet chart related to the literature focus unit or across-the-curriculum theme study, and they write the words on the sheet of butcher paper next to the appropriate letter. Students often consult the word wall and books in the theme or literature focus unit text set as they try to think of related words.

3. *Have students each choose a letter for their page.* Students consider which word they can explain best through writing and art and then sign up for that word's letter on a sheet the teacher has posted in the classroom.

4. *Design the page format.* Students consider where the letter, the illustration, and the text will be placed on the page and decide on the pattern for the text. Primary-grade students might write a single sentence of text: _____ is for _____. Middle- and upper-grade students add more information about their topics and expand the text to several sentences or a paragraph.

5. *Use the writing process to draft, revise, and edit the pages.* Then students make the final copies of the pages and add illustrations. They can handwrite the final copies or use a computer to print out professional-looking pages. Teachers also ask one student to make the cover.

6. *Compile the pages.* Students and the teacher put the pages in alphabetical order and bind the book.

APPLICATIONS AND EXAMPLES

Alphabet books are often used as projects at the end of a unit of study, such as the oceans, the desert, World War II, or California missions. The "U" page from a fourth-grade class's alphabet book on the California missions is shown in Figure 2-1.

FIGURE 2–1 The "U" Page From a Fourth-Grade Class Alphabet Book

REFERENCES

Ehlert, L. (1989). *Eating the alphabet: Fruits and vegetables from A to Z.* Orlando, FL: Harcourt Brace Jovanovich.

Hunt, J. (1989). *Illuminations.* New York: Bradbury Press.

Mullins, P. (1993). *V is for vanishing: An alphabet of endangered animals.* New York: HarperCollins.

Onyefulu, I. (1993). *A is for Africa.* New York: Dutton.

Pallotta, J. (1986). *The icky bug alphabet book.* Watertown, MA: Charlesbridge.

Tompkins, G. E. (2004). *Teaching writing: Balancing process and product* (4th ed.). Upper Saddle River, NJ: Merrill/Prentice Hall.

3

Anticipation Guides

- ● literature focus units
- ● literature circles
- ○ reading-writing workshop
- ● thematic units

- ○ preK
- ○ K–2
- ● 3–5
- ● 6–8

- ● individual
- ● pairs
- ● small group
- ● whole class

Anticipation guides (Head & Readence, 1986) are used before reading content-area textbooks and informational books to help students activate background knowledge. In an anticipation guide, teachers prepare a list of statements about the topic for students to discuss before reading. Some of the statements should be true and accurate, and others incorrect or based on common misconceptions. Students discuss each statement and decide whether they agree or disagree with it. The purpose of this activity is to stimulate students' interest in the topic and to activate background knowledge. An anticipation guide about a chapter in a social studies textbook on immigration might include these statements:

There are more people immigrating to the United States today than ever before in our history.

The government sets a quota for the number of people from each country allowed to enter the United States each year.

Most people immigrate to the United States because they want to find better jobs and earn more money.

Aliens are people who are in the United States illegally.

Refugees are people who are forced to flee from their homeland because of war or other disasters.

Many immigrants have difficulty adjusting to the new ways of life in America.

STEP BY STEP

The steps in developing an anticipation guide are:

1. *Identify several major concepts related to the reading assignment or unit.* Teachers keep in mind students' knowledge about the topic and any misconceptions they might have about it.
2. *Develop a list of four to six statements.* Teachers write statements that are general enough to stimulate discussion and can be used to clarify misconceptions. The list can be written on a chart or on a sheet of paper that is then duplicated so that students can have individual copies. The guide has space for students to mark whether or not they agree with each statement before reading and again after reading.
3. *Discuss the anticipation guide.* Teachers introduce the anticipation guide and have students respond to the statements. Working in small groups, pairs, or individually, students think about the statements and decide whether they agree or disagree with each one. Then, as a class, students discuss their responses to each statement and defend their positions.
4. *Read the text.* Students read the text and compare their responses to what is stated in the reading material.
5. *Discuss each statement again.* Students cite information in the text that supports or refutes the statement. Or, students can again respond to each of the statements and compare their answers before and after reading. When students use the anticipation guide, have them fold back their first set of responses on the left side of the paper and then respond to each item again on the right side of the paper.

APPLICATIONS AND EXAMPLES

Although anticipation guides are more commonly used to activate prior knowledge before reading in-formational books and content-area textbooks, they can also be used with novels that explore complex issues including homelessness, democratic versus totalitarian societies, crime and punishment, and immigration. One eighth-grade class, for example, studies about gangs in preparation for reading S. E. Hinton's *The Outsiders* (1967), and they complete the anticipation guide shown in Figure 3-1 before and after reading the novel. The statements about gangs in the anticipation guide probe important points and lead to lively discussion and thoughtful responses.

REFERENCES

Head, M. H., & Readence, J. E. (1986). Anticipation guides: Meaning through prediction. In E. K. Dishner, T. W. Bean, J. E. Readence, & D. W. Moore (Eds.), *Reading in the content areas* (2nd ed.) (pp. 229–234). Dubuque, IA: Kendall/Hunt.

Hinton, S. E. (1967). *The Outsiders.* New York: Viking.

Before Reading		GANGS	After Reading	
Agree	Disagree		Agree	Disagree
		1. Gangs are bad.		
		2. Gangs are exciting.		
		3. It is safe to be a gang member.		
		4. Gangs make a difference in a gang member's life.		
		5. Gangs fill a need.		
		6. Once you join a gang, it is very difficult to get out.		

FIGURE 3–1   Anticipation Guide on Gangs

Author's Chair

● literature focus units	● preK	○ individual
○ literature circles	● K–2	○ pairs
● reading-writing workshop	● 3–5	● small group
● thematic units	● 6–8	● whole class

A special chair in the classroom is designated as the author's chair. This chair might be a rocking chair, a lawn chair with a padded seat, a wooden stool, or a director's chair, and it should be labeled with a sign identifying it as the "Author's Chair" (Karelitz, 1993). Students sit in this chair to share books they have written with classmates, and this is the only time anyone sits there. Teachers at all grade levels use author's chairs, but these special chairs are most important in primary classrooms where students are developing a concept of authorship (Graves, 1994).

Donald Graves and Jane Hansen (1983) have documented children's growing awareness of authors and of themselves as authors. First, students learn that authors write books. After listening to many books read to them and after reading books themselves, children develop the concept that authors are the people who write books. Next, students realize that because they write books, they are authors, too. Sharing the books they have written with classmates from the author's chair helps children view themselves as authors. Third, students learn that they have options when they write, and this awareness grows after they have experimented with various writing purposes, forms, and audiences. After sharing their books with classmates and listening to classmates' comments, they realize that if they were to write one of their books now, they wouldn't write it the same way.

STEP BY STEP

The steps in using an author's chair are:

1. *Choose a special chair.* Teachers often purchase child-size chairs and rocking chairs at yard sales for their author's chair. Many teachers add a sign identifying the special chair as the "Author's Chair." Chairs can be painted and the sign stenciled on. Other teachers purchase director's chairs or lawn chairs to use.

2. *Explain how the author's chair will be used.* Student-authors will sit in the chair to share with classmates the books they write during writing workshop or other writing activities.

3. *Have one child sit in the author's chair.* A group of children sit on the floor or in chairs in front of the author's chair.

4. *Have the student-author read.* The child reads a book or other piece of writing aloud and shows the accompanying illustrations.

5. *Invite listeners to comment.* Students raise their hands to offer compliments, ask questions, and make other comments about the book.

6. *Have the child call on classmates.* Then after two or three students make comments about the book, the student-author chooses another child to share and takes a seat in the audience.

APPLICATIONS AND EXAMPLES

Students use the author's chair whenever they share their writing, whether it is a project completed as part of a literature focus unit or a thematic unit or as part of writing workshop. Although Graves and Hansen developed the approach for use with young children, students at all grade levels enjoy using author's chairs.

REFERENCES

Graves, D. H. (1994). *A fresh look at writing.* Portsmouth, NH: Heinemann.

Graves, D. H., & Hansen, J. (1983). The author's chair. *Language Arts, 60,* 176–183.

Karelitz, E. B. (1993). *The author's chair and beyond.* Portsmouth, NH: Heinemann.

5 Book Boxes

● literature focus units	● preK	● individual
● literature circles	● K–2	● pairs
○ reading-writing workshop	● 3–5	○ small group
● thematic units	● 6–8	○ whole class

Students decorate the outside of a box or other container and collect three to five objects or pictures related to a story, informational book, or poem and put them in the box along with a copy of the book or other reading material (Tompkins, 2003). For example, a book box for *Sarah, Plain and Tall* (MacLachlan, 1983) might include some of these objects: seashells, a train ticket, a yellow bonnet, colored pencils, a map of Sarah's trip from Maine to the prairie, and letters. Or, a book box for *The Giver* (Lowry, 1993) might include an apple, a toy bicycle, a card with the number 19, a toy sled, and a hypodermic syringe from a child's toy doctor kit. Students often make book boxes as a project after reading a book as part of a literature focus unit.

Teachers can also make book boxes to use with books they share with students. For example, a book box for *The Mitten* (Brett, 1989) might contain yarn and knitting needles, a pair of white gloves, and small stuffed animals or pictures of animals (including a mole, a snowshoe rabbit, a hedgehog, an owl, a badger, a fox, a brown bear, and a mouse). Teacher-made book boxes are especially useful for preschool and primary-grade students, students learning English as a second language, and nonverbal students who have small vocabularies and difficulty developing sentences to express ideas. By sharing a variety of objects related to the book with students before reading, teachers can build students' background knowledge and introduce vocabulary.

STEP BY STEP

The steps in preparing a book box are:

1. *Read the book.* As they read, teachers make a list of important objects mentioned in it.

2. *Choose a book box.* Teachers select a box, basket, plastic tub, empty coffee can, bag, or other container to hold the objects, and decorate it with the name of the book and related pictures and words.

3. *Fill the book box.* Teachers place three to five (or more) objects and pictures in the box along with a copy of the book. When students are making book boxes, they may include an inventory sheet with all the items listed and an explanation of why the items were selected.

4. *Share the completed box with students.* When teachers make book boxes, they use them to introduce the book and provide background information before reading. In contrast, students often make book boxes as a project after reading, and share their book boxes with classmates.

 Teachers often use book boxes with students learning English because they can teach vocabulary and build background knowledge using the objects in the boxes. As students handle and talk about the objects, they become familiar with the words and how to use them in sentences, and this preparation makes the reading experience more successful.

APPLICATIONS AND EXAMPLES

Students can also make book boxes after reading informational books and biographies. For instance, a second-grade class, after reading *Bread, Bread, Bread* (Morris, 1989), brought in sliced white bread, bagels, tortillas, pita bread, pretzels, French baguettes, cinnamon rolls, a pizza, and other kinds of bread. Students took photos of each kind of bread for their book box and marked the bread's country of origin on a world map. Then they ate the bread and wrote about their favorite kinds of bread. The teacher collected the writings, bound them into a book, and added the book to the book box, too. A fifth grader, after reading Jean Fritz's *And Then What Happened, Paul Revere?* (1973), covered a box with aluminum foil to make it look like silver and added a portrait of Paul Revere he had drawn, a strip of paper with the patriot's lifeline, a fork to symbolize the silver he made, a tea bag for the Boston Tea Party he participated in, and postcards of the Boston area that his aunt sent to him. And, when students are studying favorite authors, they can make a box with collections of the author's books, biographical information about the author, a letter the student wrote to the author, and, with luck, a response from the author.

REFERENCES

Brett, J. (1989). *The mitten.* New York: Putnam.

Fritz, J. (1973). *And then what happened, Paul Revere?* New York: Coward-McCann.

Lowry, L. (1993). *The giver.* Boston: Atheneum.

MacLachlan, P. (1983). *Sarah, plain and tall.* New York: Harper & Row.

Morris, A. (1989). *Bread, bread, bread.* New York: Scholastic.

Tompkins, G. E. (2003). *Literacy for the 21st century* (3rd ed.). Upper Saddle River, NJ: Merrill/Prentice Hall.

6 Book Talks

- ● literature focus units
- ● literature circles
- ● reading-writing workshop
- ● thematic units

- ● preK
- ● K–2
- ● 3–5
- ● 6–8

- ○ individual
- ○ pairs
- ● small group
- ● whole class

Book talks are brief teasers that teachers give to interest students in particular books. Teachers use book talks to introduce students to books in the classroom library, books for a book club, or a text set of books for a theme or written by a particular author (Gambrell & Almasi, 1996). A second-grade teacher might give a book talk to introduce various series of easy-to-read books, including Cynthia Rylant's *Henry and Mudge and the Bedtime Thumps* (1991) and other books in the Henry and Mudge series about a boy and his dog; *Fish Face* (1984) and other books in The Kids of the Polk Street School series by Patricia Reilly Giff; *Commander Toad in Space* (1980) and other books in this sci-fi series by Jane Yolen; and *Days With Frog and Toad* (1979) and other books in this award-winning series about two amphibian friends by Arnold Lobel. During the book talks, the teacher shows the books in the series, introduces the characters, and reads a short excerpt aloud to interest students in reading the books. A fifth-grade teacher might introduce five books about Harriet Tubman and the Underground Railroad and then have students form groups to read one of the books. Teachers often set books on the chalk tray after sharing them so that students can write their names on the chalkboard above the book they want to read.

STEP BY STEP

The steps in presenting a book talk are:

1. *Select one or more books to share.* When more than one book is shared, the books are usually related in some way—on the same theme, on a related topic, or written by the same author.

2. *Plan a 1- or 2-minute presentation for each book.* The presentation should include the title and author of the book, the genre or topic, and a brief summary of the plot (without giving away the ending). Teachers also explain why they liked the book and why students might be interested in it. They may also read a short excerpt and show an illustration.

3. *Show the book and present the planned book talk.* When teachers are talking about several books, they display them on a chalk tray or shelf.

APPLICATIONS AND EXAMPLES

Students use the same steps when they give a book talk, and they often give book talks when they share the books they have read during reading workshop. If students have also prepared a project related to the book, they share it during the book talk. Here is a transcript of a third grader's book talk about Paula Danziger's *Amber Brown Is Not a Crayon* (1994):

> *This is my book: Amber Brown Is Not a Crayon. It's about these two kids—Amber Brown, who is a girl, and Justin Daniels, who is a boy. See? Here is their picture. They are in third grade, too, and their teacher—his name is Mr. Cohen—pretends to take them on airplane trips to the places they study. They move their chairs so that it is like they are on an airplane and Amber and Justin always put their chairs side by side. I'm going to read you the very beginning of the book. [She reads the first three pages aloud to the class.] This story is really funny and when you are reading you think the author is telling you the story instead of you reading it. And there are more stories about Amber Brown. This is the one I'm reading now—You Can't Eat Your Chicken Pox, Amber Brown [1995].*

There are several reasons why this student and others in her class are so successful in giving book talks. The teacher has modeled how to give a book talk, and students are reading books that they have chosen—books they really like. In addition, these students are experienced in talking with their classmates about books.

REFERENCES

Danziger, P. (1994). *Amber Brown is not a crayon.* New York: Putnam.

Danziger, P. (1995). *You can't eat your chicken pox, Amber Brown.* New York: Putnam.

Gambrell, L. B., & Almasi, J. F. (Eds.). (1996). *Lively discussions! Fostering engaged reading.* Newark, DE: International Reading Association.

Giff, P. R. (1984). *Fish Face.* New York: Bantam.

Lobel, A. (1979). *Days with Frog and Toad.* New York: Harper & Row.

Rylant, C. (1991). *Henry and Mudge and the bedtime thumps.* New York: Scholastic.

Yolen, J. (1980). *Commander Toad in space.* New York: Coward-McCann.

7 Choral Reading

● literature focus units	● preK	○ individual
● literature circles	● K–2	○ pairs
● reading-writing workshop	● 3–5	● small group
● thematic units	● 6–8	● whole class

Students read aloud poems and verse using choral reading as part of literature focus units, literature circles thematic units, or reading workshop. The greatest benefit of choral reading is the shared experience of reading together (Graves, 1992; Larrick, 1991). Students may read the text aloud together as a class or divide it and read sections in small groups. Or, individual students may read particular lines or stanzas. Four possible arrangements for choral reading are:

- *Echo Reading.* A leader reads each line and the group repeats it.
- *Leader and Chorus Reading.* A leader reads the main part of the poem, and the group reads the refrain or chorus in unison.
- *Small-Group Reading.* The class divides into two or more groups, and each group reads aloud one part of the poem.
- *Cumulative Reading.* One student or one group reads the first line or stanza, and another student or group joins in as each line or stanza is read so that a cumulative effect is created.

STEP BY STEP

The steps in choral reading are:

1. *Select a poem to use for choral reading.* Teachers choose a poem or other text and copy it onto a chart or make multiple copies for students to read.
2. *Arrange the text for choral reading.* Teachers work with students to decide how to arrange the poem for reading. They add marks to the chart, or have students mark individual copies so that they can follow the arrangement.
3. *Rehearse the poem.* Teachers read the poem with students several times at a natural speed, pronouncing words carefully. Many teachers stand so that students can see how they move their mouths to form the words as they read.
4. *Have students read the poem aloud.* Teachers emphasize that students pronounce words clearly and read with expression. Teachers can tape-record students' reading so that they can hear themselves, and sometimes students want to rearrange the choral reading after hearing an audiotape of their reading.

 Choral reading is a great activity for students learning English because they practice reading aloud with classmates in a nonthreatening group setting. As they read with English-speaking classmates, they hear and practice English pronunciation of words, phrasing of words in a sentence, and intonation patterns. With practice, students' reading and oral language become more fluent.

APPLICATIONS AND EXAMPLES

Choral reading makes students active participants in the poetry experience, and it helps them learn to appreciate the sounds, feelings, and magic of poetry. Many poems can be used for choral reading, and poems with repetitions, echoes, refrains, or questions and answers work well. Try, for example:

Shel Silverstein's "Boa Constrictor"

"My Parents Think I'm Sleeping" by Jack Prelutsky

"Full of the Moon" by Karla Kuskin

Eleanor Farjeon's "Cats Sleep Anywhere"

Laura E. Richards's "Eletelephony"

"Catch a Little Rhyme" by Eve Merriam

Poems written specifically for two readers are also effective. Primary-grade students enjoy Donald Hall's book-length poem *I Am the Dog/I Am the Cat* (1994), and Paul Fleischman's collection of insect poems *Joyful Noise: Poems for Two Voices* (1988) works well with upper-grade students.

REFERENCES

Fleischman, P. (1988). *Joyful noise: Poems for two voices.* New York: Harper & Row.

Graves, D. H. (1992). *Explore poetry.* Portsmouth, NH: Heinemann.

Hall, D. (1994). *I am the dog/I am the cat.* New York: Dial.

Larrick, N. (1991). *Let's do a poem! Introducing poetry to children.* New York: Delacorte Press.

Class Collaborations

● literature focus units	● preK	○ individual
○ literature circles	● K–2	○ pairs
○ reading-writing workshop	● 3–5	● small group
● thematic units	● 6–8	● whole class

Class collaborations are books that students work together to make. Students each contribute one page or work with a classmate to write a page or a section of the book. They use the writing process as they draft, revise, and edit their pages. The benefit of collaborative books is that students share the work of creating a book so that the books are made much more quickly and easily than individual books (Tompkins, 2004). Because students write only one page or section, it takes less time for teachers to conference with students and help them to revise and edit their writing. Teachers often make class collaborations with students as a first bookmaking project and to introduce the stages of the writing process. Students at all grade levels can write collaborative books to retell a favorite story, illustrate a poem with one line or a stanza on each page, or write an informational book or biography. An alphabet book is another example of a collaborative book.

STEP BY STEP

The steps in making a collaborative book are:

 Students learning English are more likely to be successful when they write a book collaboratively than when they write independently because they work with their English-speaking classmates and thus have less writing to do so it can be completed more quickly.

1. *Choose a topic.* Teachers choose a topic related to a literature focus unit or thematic unit. Then students choose specific topics or pages to prepare.

2. *Introduce the page or section design for the book.* If students are each contributing one page for a class informational book on penguins, for example, they choose a fact or other piece of information about penguins to write. They might draw a picture related to the fact at the top of the page and write the fact underneath the picture. Teachers often model the procedure and write one page of the book together as a class before students begin working on their pages.

3. *Have students make rough drafts of their pages.* They share the pages in writing groups. Students revise their pictures and text after getting feedback from classmates. Then students correct mechanical errors and make the final copy of their pages.

4. *Compile the pages to complete the book.* Students add a title page and covers. Older students might also prepare a table of contents, an introduction, and a conclusion, and add a bibliography at the end. To make the book sturdier, teachers often laminate the covers (or all pages in the book) and have the book bound.

5. *Make copies of the book for students.* Teachers often make copies of the book for each student. The specially bound copy is often placed in the class or school library.

APPLICATIONS AND EXAMPLES

As part of literature focus units, students often retell a story or create an innovation or new version of a story in a collaborative book. They can also retell a chapter book story by having each student retell one chapter of the story. Students also can illustrate a poem or song by writing one line or stanza on each page and then drawing or painting an illustration. *The Lady With the Alligator Purse* (Westcott, 1988), *Mary*

FIGURE 8–1 A Page From a First-Grade Class Book on Johnny Appleseed

Johnny Appleseed is leaving home. He is walking on his way to the Ohio Valley. He took a sack of apple seeds and the hat on his head is really a pot. He cooks in it. He took a Bible to read and he has a stick in his hand. He has no more clothes.

Wore Her Red Dress (Peek, 1985), *Cats Sleep Anywhere* (Farjeon, 1996), and *America the Beautiful* (Bates, 1993) are four examples of song and poem retellings that have been published as picture books. These books can be used as examples for students to examine before they write their own retellings.

Students also write informational books and biographies collaboratively. For informational books, students each write a page with one fact, and for biographies, students each write about one event in the person's life. Figure 8-1 shows one page from a first-grade class book about Johnny Appleseed, written as part of a unit on apples. After the first graders wrote rough drafts, they worked with an upper-grade student to type and print out final copies of their texts.

Students can use this approach to write collaborative reports, too. Students work in small groups or with a partner to research a topic related to a thematic unit. Students often use a cluster or data chart to record the information they learn. Then students write one section of the report using information they learned through their research. They continue the writing process to revise and edit their writing. Last, they make a final copy and add their section to the class book.

REFERENCES

Bates, K. L. (1993). *America the beautiful.* New York: Atheneum.

Farjeon, E. (1996). *Cats sleep anywhere.* New York: HarperCollins.

Peek, M. (1985). *Mary wore her red dress.* New York: Clarion.

Tompkins, G. E. (2004). *Teaching writing: Balancing process and product* (4th ed.). Upper Saddle River, NJ: Merrill/Prentice Hall.

Westcott, N. B. (1988). *The lady with the alligator purse.* Boston: Little, Brown.

9 Cloze Procedure

● literature focus units	○ preK	● individual
○ literature circles	○ K–2	● pairs
○ reading-writing workshop	● 3–5	○ small group
● thematic units	● 6–8	● whole class

The cloze procedure is an informal diagnostic procedure that teachers use to gather information about readers' abilities to deal with the content and structure of texts they are reading (Taylor, 1953). Teachers construct a cloze passage by selecting an excerpt from a book—a story, an informational book, or a content-area textbook—that students have read and deleting every fifth word in the passage. The deleted words are replaced with blanks. Then students read the passage and add the missing words. Students use their knowledge of syntax (the order of words in English) and semantics (the meaning of words within sentences) to successfully predict the missing words in the text passage. Only the exact word is considered the correct answer.

Here is an example of a cloze passage about wolves:

> The leaders of a wolf pack are called the alpha wolves. There is an _____ male and an alpha _____. They are usually the _____ and the strongest wolves _____ the pack. An alpha _____ fight any wolf that _____ to take over the _____. When the alpha looks _____ other wolf in the _____, the other wolf crouches _____ and tucks its tail _____ its hind legs. Sometimes _____ rolls over and licks _____ alpha wolf's face as _____ to say, "You are _____ boss."

The missing words are *alpha, female, largest, in, will, tries, pack, the, eye, down, between, it, the, if,* and *the.*

STEP BY STEP

The steps in the cloze procedure are:

1. *Select a passage from a textbook or trade book.* The selection may be either a story or an informational piece. Then, teachers retype the passage. The first sentence is typed exactly as it appears in the original text, but beginning with the second sentence, one of the first five words is deleted and replaced with a blank. Then every fifth word in the remainder of the passage is deleted and replaced with a blank.

2. *Complete the cloze activity.* Students read the passage all the way through once silently and then reread the passage and predict or "guess" the word that goes in each blank. They write the deleted words in the blanks.

3. *Score students' work.* Teachers award one point each time the missing word is identified. A percentage of correct answers is determined by dividing the number of points by the number of blanks. Compare the percentage of correct word placements with this scale:

61% or more correct replacements	independent reading level
41–60% correct replacements	instructional level
less than 40% correct replacements	frustration level

APPLICATIONS AND EXAMPLES

The cloze procedure can be used in other ways, too. When it is used to assess students' understanding of the text, for example, specific words can be deleted, rather than every fifth word. Character names, facts related to the setting, or key events in the story can be omitted. Grading is done either by using a percentage or by giving an A for zero to two errors, a B for three to five errors, and so on.

The cloze procedure can also be used to judge whether a particular trade book or textbook is appropriate to use for classroom instruction. Teachers prepare a cloze passage and have either all students or a group of students follow the procedure described here to predict the missing words (Jacobson, 1990). Then teachers score students' predictions and use a one-third to one-half formula to determine the text's appropriateness for their students. If students correctly predict more than 50% of the deleted words, the passage is easy reading. If students predict less than 30% of the missing words, the passage is too difficult for classroom instruction. The instructional range is 30–50% correct predictions (Reutzel & Cooter, 2000).

REFERENCES

Jacobson, J. M. (1990). Group vs. individual completion of a cloze passage. *Journal of Reading, 33,* 244–250.

Reutzel, D. R., & Cooter, R. B., Jr. (2000). *Teaching children to read: From basals to books* (3rd ed.). Upper Saddle River, NJ: Merrill/Prentice Hall.

Taylor, W. L. (1953). "Cloze procedure": A new tool for measuring readability. *Journalism Quarterly, 30,* 415–433.

10 Clusters, Webs, and Maps

- literature focus units
- literature circles
- reading-writing workshop
- thematic units

- preK
- K–2
- 3–5
- 6–8

- individual
- pairs
- small group
- whole class

Clusters are spider web–like diagrams drawn on a sheet of paper. Words and phrases are written on rays drawn out from the center circle, and sometimes drawings are used instead of words or to accompany the words (Bromley, 1996; Rico, 1983). Clusters go by several names, including *webs* and *maps,* but no matter the name, they look the same and are used in the same way. Two kinds of clusters are unorganized and organized clusters. Unorganized clusters look like a child's drawing of the sun with many rays drawn out from a center circle. These clusters are most useful for brainstorming many equivalent ideas. In contrast, organized clusters are hierarchical. Several rays are drawn out from the center circle, with main ideas listed for each ray. Then more rays with details and examples are added to complete each main idea. The two kinds of clusters are shown in Figure 10–1.

STEP BY STEP

The steps in creating a cluster are:

1. *Select a topic.* Teachers and students select a topic and write the word in the center of a circle drawn on a chart or sheet of paper. The center circle can be drawn in the middle or at the top of the paper.

2. *Brainstorm a list of words.* Students brainstorm as many words and phrases that are related to the topic as they can and write them on rays drawn out from the center circle to complete an

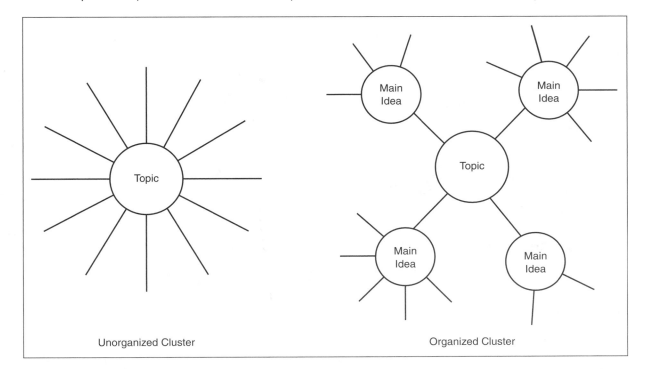

Unorganized Cluster

Organized Cluster

FIGURE 10–1 Two Kinds of Clusters

unorganized cluster. For an organized cluster, students or the teacher identifies categories, draws rays from the center circle for each category, and writes the category's name in a box or smaller circle at the end of the ray. Then students brainstorm words and phrases related to each category and write them on rays drawn out from the category box or circle.

3. *Add main ideas and details.* Students read the words and phrases recorded on the cluster, and brainstorm additional ideas to complete the cluster. The teacher may prompt students for additional words and phrases.

APPLICATIONS AND EXAMPLES

Clusters can be used in a variety of ways. Students use clusters as a tool for learning. For example, they make word clusters—unorganized clusters—and draw out rays for each of the word's meanings, and in learning logs, they make organized clusters to organize information they are learning about content-area topics, such as clouds and medieval societies. They also make clusters to organize ideas before beginning to write a composition. For a single paragraph, students often use unorganized clusters, but for longer compositions, they use organized clusters in which each main idea represents one paragraph. Teachers and students decide which type of cluster they will make depending on the topic and their purpose for making the cluster.

Students also make clusters to demonstrate their learning. Instead of writing a report, students create clusters to show what they have learned about a social studies or science topic. For example, students can make a cluster with information about a planet in the solar system, an animal, a state, or a historical event. A third-grade class's unorganized cluster about the planet Saturn is shown in Figure 10–2.

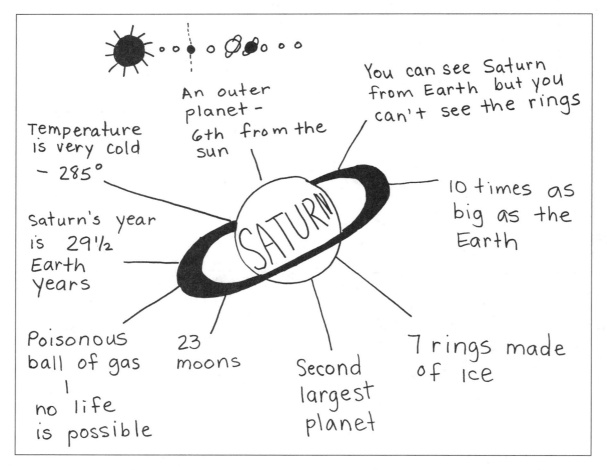

FIGURE 10–2 A Third-Grade Class's Unorganized Cluster on Saturn

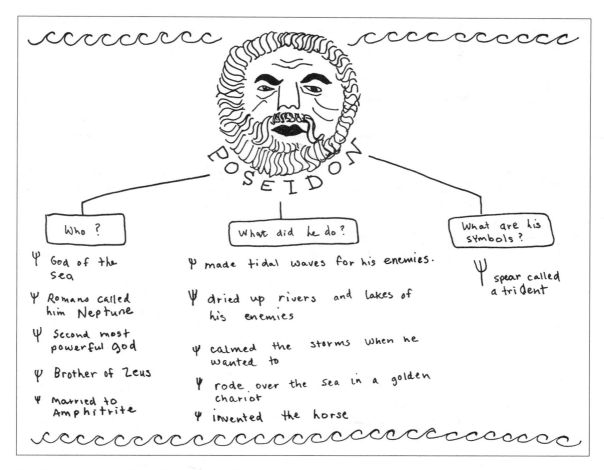

FIGURE 10–3 A Sixth Grader's Organized Cluster on Poseidon

Students also make clusters about a person's life after reading a biography or autobiography. When the clusters are used to demonstrate knowledge, students take more care to spell words correctly, use neater handwriting, and often add drawings, diagrams, and other illustrations, as shown in the sixth grader's organized cluster about Poseidon, the Greek god of the sea, in Figure 10–3.

REFERENCES

Bromley, K. D. (1996). *Webbing with literature: Creating story maps with children's books.* Boston: Allyn & Bacon.
Rico, G. L. (1983). *Writing the natural way.* Los Angeles: Tarcher.

Cubing

- ● literature focus units
- ○ literature circles
- ○ reading-writing workshop
- ● thematic units

- ○ preK
- ○ K–2
- ● 3–5
- ● 6–8

- ○ individual
- ○ pairs
- ● small group
- ● whole class

In cubing, students explore a topic from six dimensions or viewpoints (Neeld, 1986). The name "cubing" comes from the fact that cubes have six sides, just as there are six dimensions in this instructional procedure. These six dimensions are:

- Describe the topic, including its colors, shapes, and sizes.
- Compare the topic to something else. Consider how it is similar to or different from this other thing.
- Associate the topic to something else and explain why the topic makes you think of this other thing.
- Analyze the topic and tell how it is made or what it is composed of.
- Apply the topic and tell how it can be used or what can be done with it.
- Argue for or against the topic. Take a stand and list reasons to support it.

Cubes can be used in two ways: Students can create a cube as a way to review a topic they have been studying, or they can create cubes as projects to demonstrate what they have learned during a thematic unit. The first way is less formal and focuses on using cubing as a tool for learning. The second way is more formal, and students use the writing process to draft, revise, and edit their writing for each side of the cube.

STEP BY STEP

Cubing involves the following steps:

1. *Choose a topic.* Students choose a topic related to a literature focus unit or thematic unit for the cubing.
2. *Divide students into groups.* Students work in six small groups; each group examines the topic from one of the six dimensions. As an alternative, teachers divide students into six-member groups and have each group cube the topic (each member in each group will examine the topic from one of the six dimensions, and the group will create a cube).
3. *Brainstorm.* Students brainstorm ideas about the dimension and write a quickwrite or make a drawing using the ideas gathered through brainstorming.
4. *Complete the cube.* Students share their quickwrites with the class and then attach them to the sides of a box. Students can also construct a cube by folding and gluing cardboard or paper into a six-sided box, as shown in Figure 11-1.

APPLICATIONS AND EXAMPLES

Cubing is a useful procedure for across-the-curriculum thematic units, and middle- and upper-grade students can cube topics such as Antarctica, the United States Constitution, endangered animals, the Underground Railroad, and the Nile River. Students can also use cubing to explore a character in a

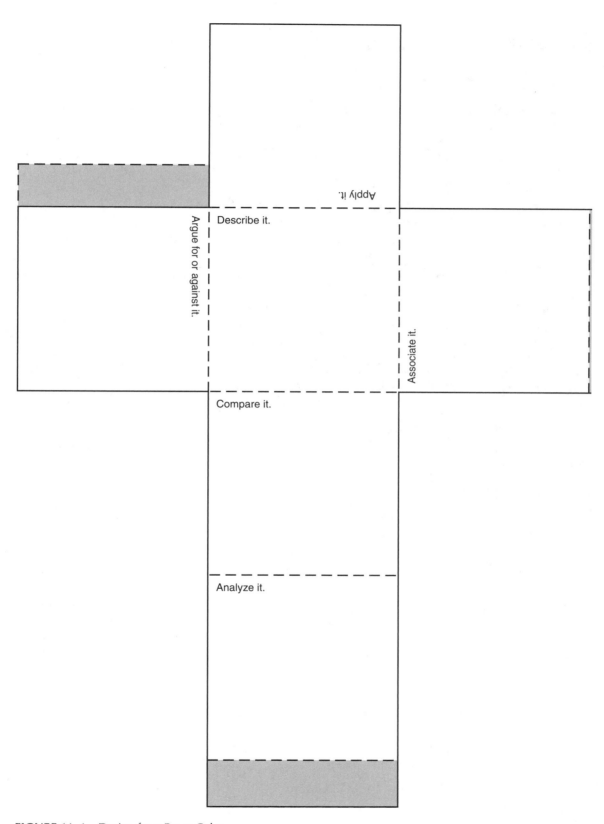

FIGURE 11–1 Design for a Paper Cube

The cube faces are labeled: Describe it., Apply it., Argue for or against it., Associate it., Compare it., Analyze it.

story. For example, a small group of fifth graders wrote this cubing about Annemarie, the Christian girl who helps to hide her Jewish friend, Ellen, in *Number the Stars* (Lowry, 1989):

Describe: Annemarie is ten years old. She is Danish and a Christian. She has silvery blond hair and blue eyes. She is smart, athletic, and a good friend to Ellen.

Compare: Annemarie is a lot like her friend Ellen. They are both Danish girls. They are both good students and good friends but they look different. Annemarie has blond hair and Ellen has brown hair. Annemarie is skinnier than Ellen and she is a better runner than Ellen. But the biggest difference is religion and what that means during World War II. Annemarie is safe because she is a Christian but Ellen is in great danger just because she is Jewish and the Germans wanted to get rid of all the Jews.

Associate: Annemarie is a lot like us. We would like her if she was in our class.

Analyze: Annemarie is just a normal girl, but she has to do some dangerous things because of the war. If there was a war in America, we might have to do dangerous things, too. We would have to be as brave as she is.

Apply: When we read about Annemarie, we learned a lot about being brave. We learned that you can't be selfish and you have to think about others. You also have to be smart and one way to be smart is to pretend to be dumb. It is better not to know too many secrets during a war.

Argue: Annemarie is the bravest person we know. She just wanted to be a girl but she had to take a stand. Ellen was brave, too, but she didn't have any choice. She would have to go to a concentration camp and probably die if she wasn't brave. Annemarie was different. She could have closed her eyes and not helped her friend, but she didn't do that because she is so brave. She made the very important choice to be brave.

REFERENCES

Lowry, L. (1989). *Number the stars.* Boston: Atheneum.

Neeld, E. C. (1986). *Writing* (2nd ed.). Glenview, IL: Scott Foresman.

12 Data Charts

● literature focus units	○ preK	● individual
○ literature circles	● K–2	● pairs
○ reading-writing workshop	● 3–5	● small group
● thematic units	● 6–8	● whole class

Data charts are grids that students make and use as a tool for organizing information about a topic (McKenzie, 1979). In literature focus units, data charts can be used to record information about versions of folktales and fairy tales, such as "Cinderella" stories, or a collection of books by an author, such as Eric Carle, Eve Bunting, and Chris Van Allsburg. In thematic units, data charts can be used to record information about the solar system, Native American tribes, and other content areas. Students also use data charts as a prewriting activity, to document what they are learning, and to categorize information.

STEP BY STEP

The steps in making a data chart are:

1. *Design the data chart.* Teachers or students choose a topic and decide how to set up the data chart with characteristics of the topic listed across the top of the chart and examples in the left column of the chart.
2. *Draw the chart.* Teachers or students create a skeleton chart on butcher paper or on a sheet of paper. They write the characteristics across the top of the chart and the examples in the left column of the chart.
3. *Complete the chart.* Students complete the chart by adding words, pictures, sentences, or paragraphs in each cell.

APPLICATIONS AND EXAMPLES

Data charts can be developed and used during literature focus units and thematic units. Students often start the chart at the beginning of the unit and then add information to the data chart as they read books or learn more about the topic. A data chart that a fifth-grade class developed during a unit on whales is shown in Figure 12–1. Small groups of students added information about the different types of whales to a large class chart, and then students used the class chart as a resource in developing individual data charts in their learning logs.

Or, students can develop a data chart in small groups or together as a class to review at the end of a unit. Another possibility is that students develop a data chart as a project at the end of a unit. Teachers can create a data chart on a bulletin board or a classroom wall. Then students divide into small groups to focus on a particular example. They write information on sheets of paper and then add the sheets of paper to complete the row for their example.

REFERENCE

McKenzie, G. R. (1979). Data charts: A crutch for helping pupils organize reports. *Language Arts, 56,* 784–788.

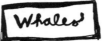

Kind	Looks	Food	Baleen or Teeth	Live
Blue Whale	largest animal 100' long blue diatoms – yellow plants on his belly	Krill	B	all oceans very rare
Narwals	10–15' gray – top white – belly dark spots all over	fish squid	T	Arctic ocean
Humpback Whales	50' long flippers black – top white – belly warts no hump!	krill and fish	B	all oceans

FIGURE 12–1   A Fifth-Grade Class Data Chart on Whales

13 Directed Reading-Thinking Activity

- ● literature focus units
- ○ literature circles
- ○ reading-writing workshop
- ○ thematic units

- ● preK
- ● K–2
- ● 3–5
- ○ 6–8

- ● individual
- ● pairs
- ● small group
- ● whole class

In the Directed Reading-Thinking Activity (DRTA), students are actively involved in reading stories or listening to stories read aloud because they make predictions and read or listen to confirm their predictions (Stauffer, 1975). DRTA is a useful approach for teaching students how to use the predicting strategy. It can be adapted and used for both picture books and chapter books.

STEP BY STEP

The steps in a DRTA lesson are:

1. *Introduce the story before beginning to read.* Teachers might discuss the topic, show objects and pictures related to the story, draw on prior knowledge, or create new experiences.

2. *Show students the cover of the book.* The teacher asks them to make a prediction about the story using these questions:

   What do you think a story with a title like this might be about?

   What do you think might happen in this story?

   Does this picture give you any ideas about what might happen in this story?

   If necessary, the teacher reads the first paragraph or two to provide more information for students to use in making their predictions. After a brief discussion in which all students commit themselves to one or another of the alternatives presented, the teacher asks these questions:

   Which of these ideas do you think would be the likely one?

   Why do you think that idea is a good one?

3. *Begin the story.* Students read the beginning of the story or listen to the beginning of the story read aloud. Then the teacher asks students to confirm or reject their predictions by responding to questions such as:

   What do you think now?

   What do you think will happen next?

   What would happen if . . . ?

   Why do you think that idea is a good one?

   Students continue reading or the teacher continues reading aloud, stopping at several key points to repeat this step.

4. *Have students reflect on their predictions.* Students talk about the story, expressing their feelings and making connections to their own lives and experiences with literature. Then students reflect on the predictions they made as they read or listened to the story read aloud, and they provide reasons to support their predictions. Teachers ask these questions to help students think about their predictions:

   What predictions did you make?

   What in the story made you think of that prediction?

   What in the story supports that idea?

FIGURE 13–1   First
Graders' Predictions About
Rosie's Walk

Predictions Before Reading *Rosie's Walk*

It's about a hen.

Maybe her name is Rosie and maybe she takes a walk.

I think she lives on the farm.

Hens lay eggs.

She could lay some eggs.

Predictions Midway Through the Story

The fox is going to catch Rosie.

I think Rosie is going to turn around and she will see the fox and she will run away real fast.

And she can fly away.

Foxes can eat gingerbread boy cookies.

Foxes like to eat foxes.

No they don't. Well, I don't think they do.

Reflections on Predictions After Reading

I'm glad Rosie didn't get eaten up.

She was very lucky. A lucky lady.

The bees chased the fox away so he couldn't eat Rosie.

I think Rosie was smart. She went to the beehives on purpose.

Yeah, that fox was dumb.

APPLICATIONS AND EXAMPLES

Teachers can write students' predictions on sentence strips or chart paper for students to reread. For example, students can make predictions about *Rosie's Walk* (Hutchins, 1968), the story of a hen named Rosie who walks around her farmyard, followed by a fox who is thwarted at every turn. Excerpts from the charts that a class of first graders developed are shown in Figure 13–1, and they illustrate how the children used DRTA to comprehend the story.

It is important to remember that DRTA is useful only when students are reading or listening to an unfamiliar story so that they can be actively involved in the prediction-confirmation cycle. When students are already familiar with the story, there is no need to ask them to make predictions.

REFERENCES

Hutchins, P. (1968). *Rosie's walk*. New York: Macmillan.
Stauffer, R. G. (1975). *Directing the reading-thinking process*. New York: Harper & Row.

14 Double-Entry Journals

- ● literature focus units
- ● literature circles
- ● reading-writing workshop
- ● thematic units

- ○ preK
- ● K–2
- ● 3–5
- ● 6–8

- ● individual
- ○ pairs
- ○ small group
- ○ whole class

A double-entry journal is a special type of reading log in which the pages are divided into two columns (Barone, 1990; Berthoff, 1981). In the left column, students write quotes from the story or informational book they are reading, and in the right column, they reflect on each quote. They may relate a quote to their own lives, react to it, write a question, or make some other connection. Excerpts from a fifth grader's double-entry journal about *The Lion, the Witch and the Wardrobe* (Lewis, 1950) are shown in Figure 14–1.

 ## STEP BY STEP

The steps in writing a double-entry journal are:

1. *Design journal pages.* Students divide the pages in their reading logs into two columns. They may label the left column "Quotes" and the right column "Comments" or "Reflections."
2. *Write quotes in journals.* As students read or immediately after reading, they copy one or more important or interesting quotes in the left column of their reading logs.

Quotes	Reflections
Chapter 1 I tell you this is the sort of house where no one is going to mind what we do.	I remember the time that I went to Beaumont, Texas to stay with my aunt. My aunt's house was very large. She had a piano and she let us play it. She told us what we could do whatever we wanted to.
Chapter 5 "How do you know?" he asked, "that your sister's story is not true?"	It reminds me of when I was little and I had an imaginary place. I would go there in my mind. I made up all kinds of make-believe stories about myself in this imaginary place. One time I told my big brother about my imaginary place. He laughed at me and told me I was silly. But it didn't bother me because nobody can stop me from thinking what I want.
Chapter 15 Still they could see the shape of the great lion lying dead in his bonds.	When Aslan died I thought about when my Uncle Carl died.
They're nibbling at the cords.	This reminds me of the story where the lion lets the mouse go and the mouse helps the lion.

FIGURE 14–1 Excerpts From a Fifth Grader's Double-Entry Journal About *The Lion, the Witch and the Wardrobe*

3. *Reflect on the quotes.* Students reread the quotes and make notes in the right column about their reasons for choosing the quote or what the quote means to them. Sometimes it is easier if students share the quotes with a reading buddy or in a grand conversation before they write comments or reflections in the right column.

APPLICATIONS AND EXAMPLES

Double-entry journals can be used in several other ways. For example, instead of recording quotes from the story, students can write "Reading Notes" in the left column and then add "Reactions" in the right column. In the left column, students write about the events they read about in the chapter. Then in the right column, they make personal connections to the events.

As an alternative, students can use the heading "Reading Notes" for one column and "Discussion Notes" for the second column. Students write reading notes as they read or immediately after reading. Later, after discussing the story or chapter of a longer book, students add discussion notes. As with other types of double-entry journals, it is the second column in which students make more interpretive comments.

Younger students can use the double-entry format for a prediction journal (Macon, Bewell, & Vogt, 1991). They label the left column "Predictions" and the right column "What Happened." In the left column, they write or draw a picture of what they predict will happen in the story or chapter before reading it. Then after reading, they draw or write what actually happened in the right column.

REFERENCES

Barone, D. (1990). The written responses of young children: Beyond comprehension to story understanding. *The New Advocate, 3,* 49–56.

Berthoff, A. E. (1981). *The making of meaning.* Montclair, NJ: Boynton/Cook.

Lewis, C. S. (1950). *The lion, the witch and the wardrobe.* New York: Macmillan.

Macon, J. M., Bewell, D., & Vogt, M. E. (1991). *Responses to literature: Grades K–8.* Newark, DE: International Reading Association.

15 Exclusion Brainstorming

○ literature focus units	○ preK	○ individual
○ literature circles	○ K–2	● pairs
○ reading-writing workshop	● 3–5	● small group
● thematic units	● 6–8	● whole class

Exclusion brainstorming is a prereading activity that teachers use to activate students' prior knowledge and expand their understanding about a social studies or science topic before reading (Blachowicz, 1986). Teachers present students with a list of words to read, and students identify words on the list that relate to the topic as well as those that do not belong. As they talk about the words and try to decide which words are related to the topic, students refine their knowledge of the topic, are introduced to some key vocabulary words, and develop a purpose for reading. Then after reading, students review the list of words and decide whether or not they chose the words correctly.

STEP BY STEP

The steps in exclusion brainstorming are:

1. *Prepare a word list.* Teachers identify words related to an informational book or content-area textbook that students will read and include a few words that do not fit with the topic. They write the list on the chalkboard or on an overhead transparency, or make copies for students.

2. *Read the list of words with students.* Then, in small groups or together as a class, students decide which words are related to the text and which words are not related. They draw circles around words that they think are not related.

3. *Learn about the topic.* Students read the assignment, noticing whether the words in the exclusion brainstorming exercise are mentioned in the text.

4. *Check the list.* After reading, students check their exclusion brainstorming list and make corrections based on their reading. They put check marks by related words and cross out unrelated words, whether they circled them earlier or not.

APPLICATIONS AND EXAMPLES

Teachers use exclusion brainstorming as a prereading activity to familiarize students with key concepts and vocabulary before they read informational books and articles. An eighth-grade teacher, for example, prepared the list of words shown in Figure 15–1 before his students read an article on the Arctic Ocean. All of the words except *penguins, South Pole,* and *precipitation* were related to the Arctic Ocean. Students circled seven words as possibly unrelated, and after reading, they crossed out the same three words that their teacher expected them to eliminate.

Exclusion brainstorming can also be used with stories when teachers want to focus on a social studies or science concept before reading the story. A fourth-grade teacher created the exclusion brainstorming list shown in Figure 15–2 before reading *The Ballad of Lucy Whipple* (Cushman, 1996), the story of a young girl who travels with her family to California during the gold rush. The teacher used this activity to introduce some of the vocabulary in the story and to help students develop an understanding of life during the California gold rush. Students circled seven words before reading, and after reading, they crossed out three words, all different from the ones they had circled earlier.

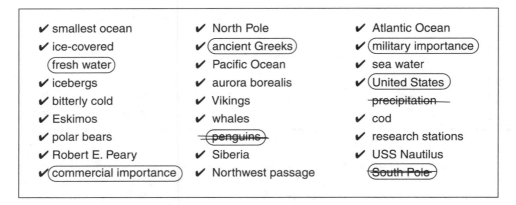

FIGURE 15–1   An Exclusion Brainstorming About the Arctic Ocean

FIGURE 15–2   An Exclusion Brainstorming About *The Ballad of Lucy Whipple*

REFERENCES

Blachowicz, C. L. Z. (1986). Making connections: Alternatives to the vocabulary notebook. *Journal of Reading, 29,* 643–649.

Cushman, K. (1996). *The ballad of Lucy Whipple.* New York: Clarion Books.

16 Gallery Walk

- ● literature focus unit
- ○ literature circles
- ● reading-writing workshop
- ● thematic units

- ○ preK
- ● K–2
- ● 3–5
- ● 6–8

- ○ individual
- ○ pairs
- ● small groups
- ● whole class

Students move around the classroom during a gallery walk to view, read, and respond to classmates' work. Usually the work is displayed on the walls of the classroom, but it can also be placed on students' desks. Classmates respond by writing comments and questions on little sticky notes and attaching them to the edge of the student's work or by drawing or writing comments on a "graffiti board" (a sheet of paper) posted next to each student's work. Kindergartners, for example, might view classmates' paintings, or second graders might view classmates' photographs and read their accompanying sentences or paragraphs. Fifth graders might view classmates' maps of the American colonies or clusters they have made about a state or an animal. Middle school students might share idiom posters with literal and figurative meanings that they have created or copies of letters to the editor of the local newspaper that they have written and already sent to the newspaper office.

Students' work can be completed or in progress. When the work has been completed, a gallery walk is a celebration, much like the author's chair (see p. 9). For example, first graders might set books they have published during writing workshop on their desks and classmates move around the classroom, stopping at each child's desk to read the book and write a comment on the comments page in the back of the book. When the work is in progress, a gallery walk functions much like a writing group to provide feedback and suggestions to authors. For example, sixth graders might post copies of drafts of poems for classmates to read and highlight favorite lines in the poems.

A gallery walk provides an immediate audience for students' writing projects. The activity can be completed much more quickly than if each student were to share his or her work in front of the class, and because classmates will view their work, students are often more motivated than when the teacher will be the only audience. In addition, students provide supportive feedback through their responses to their classmates, and they learn new ideas they can incorporate in their own writing projects.

STEP BY STEP

The steps in conducting a gallery walk are:

1. *Display the work.* Students and the teacher post the work on classroom walls or place it on desks in preparation for the gallery walk.

2. *Provide comment sheets.* Teachers give students small sticky notes on which to write comments or place graffiti sheets next to each student's work.

3. *Give directions for the gallery walk.* Teachers explain the purpose of the gallery walk, how to view and/or read the work, and what comments to make to classmates. Teachers also set time limits and direct students to visit three, five, eight, or more students' work, if there is not time to read everyone's work.

4. *Model how to view, read, and respond.* The teacher models how to behave during the gallery walk using one or two students' work as examples.

5. *Direct the flow of traffic.* Teachers direct students as they move around the classroom, making sure that all students' work is viewed, read, and responded to and that comments are supportive and useful.

6. *Bring closure to the gallery walk.* Teachers ask students to move to their own art or writing projects and look at the comments, questions, or other responses they have received. Often one or two students will share their responses or comment on the gallery walk experience.

APPLICATIONS AND EXAMPLES

A good way to introduce a gallery walk is to post pictures and have students move around the classroom, writing what a picture makes them think of on small sticky notes, which they attach under the picture. This first experience is not threatening because students' work is not being critiqued, but after this experience, students need to respond to classmates' art and writing because having an audience for their work is the purpose behind the gallery walk activity.

After students learn to make positive, supportive comments about classmates' work, they can also try writing questions after reading classmates' rough drafts to assist classmates in revising their writing. Students read the rough drafts and then write questions asking classmates to clarify, rephrase, or extend an idea. For example, after reading a fourth grader's rough draft report about volcanoes, students asked:

> What does *magna* mean?
> Are there any volcanoes in California?
> Can you add *first, second,* and *third* for the sequence?
> What is your title?
> Are mountains and volcanoes the same thing?
> What starts the fire in the volcano?
> Are any volcanoes exploding today?

Questions like these provide direction for students as they revise their writing.

17

Goldilocks Strategy

○ literature focus units   ○ preK   ● individual
● literature circles   ● K–2   ○ pairs
● reading-writing workshop   ● 3–5   ○ small group
○ thematic units   ● 6–8   ○ whole class

Students use the Goldilocks Strategy (Ohlhausen & Jepsen, 1992) to select books to read independently. Goldilocks in "The Three Bears" folktale classified the porridge as "too hot," "too cold," and "just right." Similarly, books that students read can be categorized as "too hard," "too easy," or "just right." Books in the "too hard" category may include books that are confusing and have many unfamiliar words, small type, and few illustrations. "Too easy" books are books that students have read before or can read fluently, and "just right" books are interesting, with just a few unfamiliar words. The books in each category vary according to each student's reading level.

The Goldilocks Strategy can be used by students at any grade level, kindergarten through eighth grade, because of the way the characteristics are stated. A third-grade class developed the Goldilocks Strategy chart shown in Figure 17–1, but the characteristics might be worded differently by students at other grade levels.

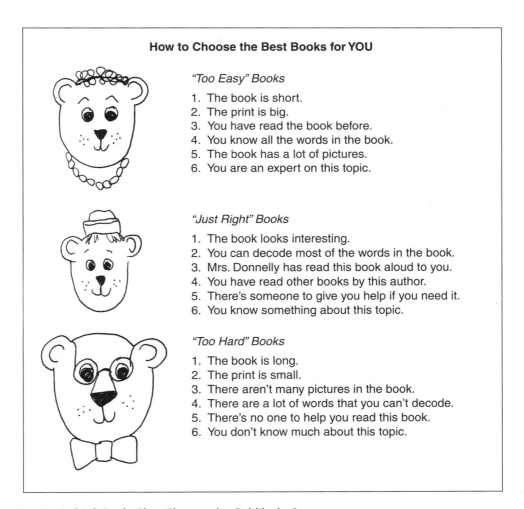

How to Choose the Best Books for YOU

"Too Easy" Books

1. The book is short.
2. The print is big.
3. You have read the book before.
4. You know all the words in the book.
5. The book has a lot of pictures.
6. You are an expert on this topic.

"Just Right" Books

1. The book looks interesting.
2. You can decode most of the words in the book.
3. Mrs. Donnelly has read this book aloud to you.
4. You have read other books by this author.
5. There's someone to give you help if you need it.
6. You know something about this topic.

"Too Hard" Books

1. The book is long.
2. The print is small.
3. There aren't many pictures in the book.
4. There are a lot of words that you can't decode.
5. There's no one to help you read this book.
6. You don't know much about this topic.

FIGURE 17–1   A Third-Grade Class Chart on the Goldilocks Strategy

When students learn to use the Goldilocks Strategy, they can choose books at their own reading level and can assume more responsibility for choosing their own books for reading workshop or other independent reading time. In addition, they are more likely to read more and to enjoy reading than those students who don't choose books at an appropriate level of difficulty or who are assigned books to read.

STEP BY STEP

The steps in using the Goldilocks Strategy are:

1. *Introduce the Goldilocks Strategy.* Teachers explain that the Goldilocks Strategy is a procedure that students use to select books during reading workshop. They share three books with students and talk about the books they like to read themselves. They share a book that is too easy for them (e.g., a book written for young children), a book that is too hard (e.g., an automotive repair book, directions for knitting a sweater, or a college textbook), and a book that is just right (e.g., a novel). Teachers emphasize that everyone has books that fit into these three categories.

2. *Analyze books.* Teachers talk with students about the books that are too easy, too hard, and just right for them, and students identify some of the characteristics of each type. Next teachers create a class chart with students listing the characteristics of books that are too hard, too easy, and just right. They post the chart in the library center of the classroom and encourage students to use the strategy when selecting books.

3. *Have students apply the strategy.* Teachers ask students to use the three categories when they discuss books they are reading. For example, a second grader was flipping through the pages of *Tales of a Fourth Grade Nothing* (Blume, 1972) during reading workshop, and her teacher walked over to her and asked her if she was enjoying the book. The girl responded, "I think this is too hard. My sister just read it and she said it was really good. But I just know some of the words—like *television.* It's a big word but I know it. I guess it is a 'too hard' book, but I wanted to read it." And, a seventh grader said this during a conference with his teacher: "I just finished rereading this book—*Hatchet* [Paulsen, 1987]. We read it in Mr. Dodd's class last year and when I saw it on the shelf I just wanted to read it again. I guess you could call it a 'too easy' book because I had read it before and it wasn't hard for me to read, but it was good and I liked it even better this time."

APPLICATIONS AND EXAMPLES

Students use these three categories as they select books in the classroom library and the school library and as they talk about the books they are reading in conferences with the teacher. Students can also code the books in their reading logs according to the three categories using the initials TH for "too hard," TE for "too easy," and JR for "just right."

REFERENCES

Blume, J. (1972). *Tales of a fourth grade nothing.* New York: Dutton.
Ohlhausen, M. M., & Jepsen, M. (1992). Lessons from Goldilocks: "Someone has been choosing my books but I can make my own choices now!" *The New Advocate, 5,* 31–46.
Paulsen, G. (1987). *Hatchet.* New York: Viking.

18 Grand Conversations

- ● literature focus units
- ● literature circles
- ○ reading-writing workshop
- ○ thematic units

- ● preK
- ● K–2
- ● 3–5
- ● 6–8

- ○ individual
- ○ pairs
- ● small group
- ● whole class

A grand conversation is a discussion about a book in which students explore interpretations and reflect on their feelings (Eeds & Wells, 1989; Peterson & Eeds, 1990). Students sit in a circle so that they can see each other. Teachers serve as facilitators, but the talk is primarily among the students. Traditionally, literature discussions have been "gentle inquisitions"; here the talk changes to dialoguing among students.

STEP BY STEP

The steps in conducting a grand conversation are:

1. *Read the book.* Students read the book or part of the book, or they listen to the teacher read it aloud.

2. *Prepare for the grand conversation.* Students respond to the book in a quickwrite (or quickdraw for younger students) or in a reading log. This step is optional.

3. *Discuss the book.* Students get together as a class or in smaller groups to discuss the book.

4. *Share ideas.* Students take turns sharing their ideas about the book (the story, personal connections to the story, the language, the illustrations, and the author/illustrator). To start the grand conversation, the teacher asks students to share their ideas and to ask questions. Possible openers are "Who would like to begin?" "What did you think?" and "Who would like to share?" They may read from their quickwrites or reading log entries. Students each participate and may build on classmates' comments and ask for clarifications. In order that everyone may participate, students should not make more than two or three comments until everyone has spoken once. Students may refer back to the book or read a short piece to make a point, but there is no round-robin reading. Pauses may occur, and when students indicate that they have run out of things to say, the grand conversation may end or continue in a second part.

5. *Ask questions.* Teachers ask open-ended questions after students have had a chance to share their reflections. These questions should focus students' attention on one or two aspects of the book that have not yet been mentioned. Teachers might focus on the illustrations, the author, or literary elements, or compare the book with another book or a video version of the book.

6. *Reflect on the conversation.* Students write (or write again) a quickwrite or in a reading log. This step is optional.

APPLICATIONS AND EXAMPLES

Grand conversations take only 10 to 20 minutes and can be done after a book or after every chapter (or section) of a longer book. It is not necessary to grade students' participation in grand conversations, but students are expected to make comments and be supportive of classmates' contributions. Also, students can write a brief entry in reading logs before the grand conversation and then write a second entry describing what they learned during the grand conversation.

REFERENCES

Eeds, M., & Wells, D. (1989). Grand conversations: An exploration of meaning construction in literature study groups. *Research in the Teaching of English, 22,* 4–29.

Peterson, R., & Eeds, M. (1990). *Grand conversations: Literature groups in action.* New York: Scholastic.

19 Guided Reading

- ● literature focus units
- ○ literature circles
- ○ reading-writing workshop
- ○ thematic units

- ○ preK
- ● K–2
- ● 3–5
- ○ 6–8

- ○ individual
- ○ pairs
- ● small group
- ○ whole class

Teachers use guided reading to read a book with a small group of students who read at approximately the same reading level (Clay, 1991). They select a book that students can read at their instructional level, that is, with approximately 90–94% accuracy. Teachers use the reading process and support students' reading and their use of reading strategies during guided reading (Depree & Iversen, 1996; Fountas & Pinnell, 1996). Students do the actual reading themselves, and they usually read silently at their own pace through the entire book. Emergent readers often mumble the words softly as they read, and this helps the teacher keep track of students' reading and the strategies they are using. Guided reading is not round-robin reading, in which students take turns reading pages aloud to the group.

During guided reading, students read books that they have not read before. Emergent readers usually read small picture books at one sitting, but older students who are reading longer chapter books take several days to several weeks to read them.

STEP BY STEP

The steps in guided reading are:

1. *Choose an appropriate book for the small group of students.* The students should be able to read the book with 90–94% accuracy. Teachers collect copies of the book for each student in the group.

2. *Introduce the book to the group.* Teachers show the cover, reading the title and author, and activating students' prior knowledge on a topic related to the book. They often use key vocabulary as they talk about the book, but they don't use vocabulary flash cards to drill students on new words before reading. Students also "picture walk" through the book, looking at the illustrations and talking about them.

3. *Have students read the book independently.* Teachers provide support to students with decoding and reading strategies as needed. Students either read silently or "mumble" read softly. Teachers observe students as they read and assess their use of word-identification and comprehension strategies. They help individual students decode unfamiliar words, deal with unfamiliar sentence structures, and comprehend ideas presented in the text whenever assistance is required.

4. *Provide opportunities for students to respond to the book.* Students talk about the book, ask questions, and relate it to others they have read, as in a grand conversation.

5. *Involve students in one or two exploring activities.* Examples:

    teach a phonics concept, word-identification skill, or reading strategy

    review vocabulary words

    examine an element of story structure

6. *Provide opportunities for independent reading.* Teachers place the book in a book basket or in the classroom library so that students can reread it independently during reading workshop.

APPLICATIONS AND EXAMPLES

Students move through the reading process as they read in small guided reading groups. Figure 19–1 shows an instructional plan for two books. In the first book, *Where's Little Mole?* (Greene, 1994), Mrs. Mole goes looking for her son and a series of animals that live underground respond that "he's not here." At the end of the brief story, the little mole scurries through a tunnel in the burrow to find his mother. This little book for emergent readers has seven pages, with one sentence of text on each page. The second book is *Sideways Stories From Wayside School* (Sachar, 1978), a series of 30 brief chapters about the teacher and students on the 30th floor of Wayside School. Each chapter is a description of one of the students or their teacher. This book is written at the third-grade reading level, and its very brief chapters make it suitable for less fluent readers. In Figure 19–1, brief descriptions of the teaching plan are shown for each of the five stages of the reading process (Tompkins, 2003).

REFERENCES

Clay, M. M. (1991). *Becoming literate: The construction of inner control.* Portsmouth, NH: Heinemann.

Depree, H., & Iversen, S. (1996). *Early literacy in the classroom: A new standard for young readers.* Bothell, WA: Wright Group.

Fountas, I. C., & Pinnell, G. S. (1996). *Guided reading: Good first teaching for all children.* Portsmouth, NH: Heinemann.

Greene, I. (1994). *Where's little mole?* Glenview, IL: Good Year Books.

Sachar, L. (1978). *Sideways stories from Wayside School.* New York: Avon Books.

Sachar, L. (1993). *Wayside School is falling down.* New York: Avon Books.

Tompkins, G. E. (2003). *Literacy for the 21st century* (3rd ed.). Upper Saddle River, NJ: Merrill/Prentice Hall.

Stage of the Reading Process	Where's Little Mole?	Sideways Stories From Wayside School
Prereading	The teacher displays a puppet of a mole, talks briefly about moles, and asks students to name other animals that live underground. The teacher shows the cover of the book and reads the title and author. Students "picture walk" through the book, identifying the underground animals in the illustrations and noticing that Little Mole is just out of his mother's sight in each illustration.	The teacher introduces the book to students by reading aloud the Introduction on page 9. Then students look at the picture on the cover and make predictions about the unusual school and the students and teacher on the 30th floor.
Reading	Students read the first two pages aloud with the teacher. Then students mumble read the story independently while the teacher observes and provides assistance as needed.	Each day, students read two or three chapters silently while the teacher provides assistance as needed. The teacher emphasizes the importance of the visualization strategy when reading about the characters.
Responding	Students talk about the story, and the teacher asks students if they think Mrs. Mole found her child or if Little Mole found his mother.	Students talk about the characters they have read about. They ask clarifying questions and compare the characters to themselves and other children they know.
Exploring	Students read sentence strips on which the sentences from the story have been written. Then they cut the sentence strips apart into words and arrange them into sentences. Then the teacher reviews the CVCe long-vowel pattern using *mole* as an example, and students write a list of CVCe words on white boards. Examples: *mole, late, mule, lime,* and *pine.*	Students each make a grid with 30 spaces on the inside of a file folder. After reading about each chapter, they draw a sketch of the character introduced in the chapter and write descriptive words and phrases to help visualize that character. The teacher reviews descriptive words with students and helps them differentiate between essential and nonessential attributes for each character.
Applying	Students reread the story with buddies, and then a copy of the book is put into the reading baskets on each grouping of desks in the classroom for students to reread independently.	After reading the book, the teacher places several copies of the book in the classroom library and encourages students to reread the book during reading workshop. The teacher also introduces the sequel, *Wayside School Is Falling Down* (Sachar, 1993), and invites students to read it independently.

FIGURE 19–1   Plans for Teaching Two Stories Using Guided Reading

20 Instructional Conversations

- ◯ literature focus units
- ◯ literature circles
- ◯ reading-writing workshop
- ● thematic units

- ● preK
- ● K–2
- ● 3–5
- ● 6–8

- ◯ individual
- ◯ pairs
- ● small group
- ● whole class

Instructional conversations are like grand conversations except that they are about nonfiction topics, not about literature. These conversations provide opportunities for students to talk about the main ideas they are learning in content-area units and enhance both students' conceptual learning and their linguistic abilities (Goldenberg, 1992/1993). Like grand conversations, these discussions are interesting and engaging, and students are active participants, building on classmates' ideas with their own comments. Teachers are participants in the conversation, making comments much like the students do, but they also assume the teacher role to clarify misconceptions, ask questions, and provide instruction. Goldenberg has identified these content and linguistic elements of an instructional conversation:

- The conversation focuses on a content-area topic.
- Students activate or build knowledge about the topic during the instructional conversation.
- Teachers provide information and directly teach concepts when necessary.
- Teachers promote students' use of more complex vocabulary and language to express the ideas being discussed.
- Teachers encourage students to provide support for the ideas they present using information presented in content-area textbooks, text sets, and other unit-related resources in the classroom.
- Students and teachers ask higher-level questions, often questions with more than one answer, during the instructional conversation.
- Students participate actively in the instructional conversation and make comments that build upon and expand classmates' comments.
- The classroom is a community of learners where both students' and teachers' comments are respected and encouraged.

STEP BY STEP

The steps in an instructional conversation are:

1. *Choose a focus.* Teachers choose a focus for the instructional conversation. It should be related to the goals of a content-area unit or main ideas presented in an informational book or in a content-area textbook.

2. *Prepare for the instructional conversation.* Teachers present background knowledge in preparation for the discussion, or students may read an informational book or selection from a content-area textbook to learn about the topic.

3. *Begin the conversation.* Students come together as a class or in a smaller group for the instructional conversation. Teachers begin with the focus they have identified. They make a statement or ask a question, and then students respond, sharing information they have learned, asking questions, and offering opinions. Teachers assist students as they make comments, helping them extend their ideas and use appropriate vocabulary. In addition, teachers write students' comments in a list or on a cluster or other graphic organizer.

4. *Expand the conversation.* After students have discussed the teacher's focus, the conversation continues and moves in other directions. Students may share other interesting information,

make personal connections to information they are learning, or ask questions. Teachers may also want to have students do a read-around and share important ideas from their reading.

5. *Write in learning logs.* Students write and draw in learning logs and record the important ideas discussed during the instructional conversation. Students may refer to the brainstormed list or cluster that the teacher made during the first part of the discussion.

APPLICATIONS AND EXAMPLES

Instructional conversations are useful for helping students grapple with important ideas they are learning in thematic units. For example, during a unit on immigration, a class of fifth graders interview their parents to find out if they are immigrants or descendants of immigrants, write summaries of their interviews, and share what they learned with their classmates. Next, students read a chapter in their social studies textbook about America being a land of immigrants. Then the teacher brings the class together to have an instructional conversation. The teacher begins by writing *The United States is a nation of immigrants* on the chalkboard, reads the statement aloud, and asks the students what they think the statement means. The children share what they have learned through the interviews they conducted with their parents and through reading the textbook chapter. As the children talk about immigrants, the teacher reviews the terms *immigrants* and *descendants* and reinforces the three main concepts from the textbook chapter through these statements and follow-up questions:

Main idea #1: People from many nations have come to the United States

So, we know that everyone in our class is an immigrant or a descendant of immigrants. Lots of our families came from Mexico, but did other families come from other countries?

We know that immigrants come to the United States from Mexico, Cambodia, England, Russia, Pakistan, China, and Italy. Can you think of any other countries?

Main idea #2: Reasons why the immigrants came

We know that immigrants come to America for different reasons. What are some of these reasons?

Yes, I agree. Sometimes people come to America so that they have a good job and earn money to support their families. Are there some other reasons?

Do you remember the story *Molly's Pilgrim*? Why did Molly's family come to America?

What about the Pilgrims who came on the Mayflower in 1620? Why did they come?

Famine. That's an interesting word. What does it mean? So why do people come to America when there is a famine in their country?

We've talked about coming to the United States for religious freedom, for jobs and safety, and to escape war and famine. Do you think these immigrants were happy or sad to leave their own countries?

Main idea #3: The arduous journey to America

So, we know that many, many immigrants are coming to America. What I'm wondering is how do the immigrants get here?

What about the immigrants from Viet Nam and China? They can't get in a car and drive to America because of the Pacific Ocean. How could they travel to the United States?

Are the trips to America easy for the immigrants? Why not? What could happen on the trip?

As the students talk about the statement the teacher wrote on the chalkboard, their conversation jumps from idea to idea, but the teacher redirects the conversation by asking a question or making a statement. After students talk about the three main points, the teacher asks the students each to say an important idea that they remember about immigrants, either from their reading or from the discussion. The students' comments include:

> Some people come to America because there is a war in their country and they want to be safe.
>
> Everyone in our class is an immigrant.
>
> Pilgrims were immigrants so they had the first Thanksgiving because they were thankful to be in America.
>
> Immigrants come from all over the world.
>
> America is a better country because there are immigrants.
>
> I think most of the immigrants come from Mexico.
>
> In America you can be any religion your parents want and that is a good thing.
>
> I thought that the white people were always in America, but now I know that only the Indians are original.
>
> Some people come to America in a car and some people come in a boat or in a plane.
>
> People cry when they leave their home to come to America because they love their country but they have to leave.

To conclude the instructional conversation, students write a quickwrite response to the statement on the chalkboard. Here is one fifth grader's response:

> *People love America and they come to have a new life here when things get bad where they live. They are called immigrants. They are sad to leave but happy to be safe in the U.S.A. The U.S.A. is full of immigrants and it is good because they make America good. My dad is an immigrant. He came to the U.S.A. from Mexico. My mom, me, and my brothers are descendants. We are part Mexico and part U.S.A. I wish my uncle could be an immigrant, too, but he wants to stay in Mexico. He probably will come if there is a war or the police say he cannot go to church.*

This student addresses the main ideas in his quickwrite and makes personal connections to the topic. In addition, he weaves the two vocabulary words—*immigrant* and *descendant*—into his quickwrite. This writing sample demonstrates that the student understands that the United States is a nation of immigrants.

REFERENCE

Goldenberg, C. (1992/1993). Instructional conversations: Promoting comprehension through discussion. *The Reading Teacher, 46,* 316–326.

21 Interactive Writing

- ● literature focus units
- ○ literature circles
- ○ reading-writing workshop
- ● thematic units

- ○ preK
- ● K–2
- ○ 3–5
- ○ 6–8

- ○ individual
- ○ pairs
- ● small group
- ● whole class

In interactive writing, students and the teacher create a text and "share the pen" as they write the text on chart paper (Button, Johnson, & Furgerson, 1996). The text is composed by the group, and the teacher guides students as they write the text word-by-word on chart paper. Students take turns writing known letters and familiar words, adding punctuation marks, and marking spaces between words. All students participate in creating and writing the text on chart paper, and they also write the text on small white boards. After writing, students read and reread the text using shared reading and independent reading.

Interactive writing is used to show students how writing works and how to construct words using their knowledge of sound-symbol correspondences and spelling patterns. This instructional strategy was developed by the well-known English educator Moira McKenzie, who based it on Don Holdaway's work in shared reading (Fountas & Pinnell, 1996).

STEP BY STEP

The steps in interactive writing are:

1. *Collect materials for interactive writing.* Teachers collect chart paper, colored marking pens, white correction tape, an alphabet chart, magnetic letters or letter cards, and a pointer. They also collect these materials for individual students' writing: small white boards, dry-erase pens, and erasers.

2. *Set a purpose for the activity.* Teachers present a stimulus activity or set a purpose for the interactive writing activity. Often they read or reread a trade book as a stimulus, but students also can write daily news, compose a letter, or brainstorm information they are learning in social studies or science.

3. *Choose a sentence to write.* Teachers negotiate the text—often a sentence or two—with students. Students repeat the sentence several times and segment the sentence into words. The teacher also helps the students remember it as it is written.

4. *Pass out writing supplies.* Teachers distribute individual white boards, dry-erase pens, and erasers for students to use to write the text individually as it is written together as a class on chart paper. They periodically ask students to hold their white boards up so they can see what the students are writing.

Interactive writing is a useful technique for students learning to write, whether they are kindergartners or older children who are learning to speak English and read and write at the same time. Teachers use the same procedure for English learners that they use with young children: They help the students negotiate a sentence and write it in standard English. Teachers take advantage of opportunities to reinforce English pronunciation, spelling rules, sentence structure, and conventions of print.

5. *Write the first sentence word-by-word.* Before writing the first word, the teacher and students slowly pronounce the word, "pulling" it from their mouths or "stretching" it out. Then students take turns writing the letters in the first word. The teacher chooses students to write each sound or the entire word, depending on students' knowledge of phonics and spelling. Teachers often have students use one color of pen for the letters they write, and they use another color and write the parts of words that students don't know how to spell. In that way, teachers can keep track of how much writing students are able to do. Teachers keep a poster with the upper- and lowercase letters of the alphabet to refer to when students are unsure about how to form a

letter, and they use white correction tape (sometimes called "boo-boo" tape) when students write a letter incorrectly or write the wrong letter. After writing each word, one student serves as the "spacer"; this student uses his or her hand to mark the space between words and sentences. Teachers have students reread the sentence from the beginning each time a new word is completed. When appropriate, teachers call children's attention to capital letters, punctuation marks, and other conventions of print. They repeat this procedure to write additional sentences to complete the text. When teachers use interactive writing to write a class collaboration book (see p. 17), this activity can take several days or a week or longer to complete.

6. *Display the interactive writing.* After the writing is completed, teachers post the chart in the classroom and have students reread the text using shared or independent reading. Students often reread interactive charts when they "read the room." They may also add artwork to "finish" the chart.

APPLICATIONS AND EXAMPLES

Interactive writing can be used as part of literature focus units, in social studies and science thematic units, and for many other purposes, too. Some uses are:

Write predictions before reading

Write responses after reading

Write letters and other messages

Make lists

Write daily news

Rewrite a familiar story

Write information or facts

Write recipes

Make K-W-L charts, clusters, data charts, and other diagrams

Create innovations, or new versions of a familiar text

Write class poems

Write words on a word wall

Make posters

When students begin interactive writing in kindergarten, they write letters to represent the beginning sounds in words and write familiar words such as *the, a,* and *is.* The first letters that students write are often the letters in their own names, particularly the first letter. As students learn more about sound-symbol correspondences and spelling patterns, they do more of the writing. Once students are writing words fluently, they can continue to do interactive writing as they work in small groups. Each student in the group uses a particular color pen and takes turns writing letters, letter clusters, and words. They also get used to using the white correction tape, and use it to correct poorly formed letters and misspelled words. Students also sign their names in color on the page so that the teacher can track which student wrote which words. A black-and-white copy of a small group's interactive active writing about snails is shown in Figure 21–1. The boxes around two letters and one word represent the white correction tape that students used.

REFERENCES

Button, K., Johnson, M. J., & Furgerson, P. (1996). Interactive writing in a primary classroom. *The Reading Teacher, 49,* 446–454.

Fountas, I. C., & Pinnell, G. S. (1996). *Guided reading: Good first teaching for all children.* Portsmouth, NH: Heinemann.

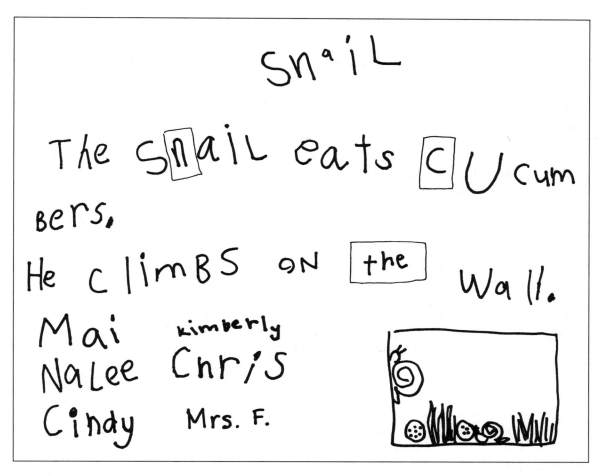

FIGURE 21–1 A Small Group's Interactive Writing About Snails

22

K-W-L Chart

○ literature focus units   ○ preK   ● individual
○ literature circles   ● K–2   ● pairs
○ reading-writing workshop   ● 3–5   ● small group
● thematic units   ● 6–8   ● whole class

Teachers use K-W-L charts during across-the-curriculum thematic units to activate students' background knowledge about a topic and to assist students in generating questions and organizing information they are learning (Ogle 1986, 1989). Teachers create a K-W-L chart by hanging up three sheets of butcher paper or dividing chart paper and labeling the sections *K, W,* and *L;* the letters stand for "What We **K**now," "What We **W**onder" or "What We **W**ant to Learn," and "What We **L**earned." A partially completed K-W-L chart developed by a kindergarten class as they were hatching chicks is shown in Figure 22–1. The teacher did the actual writing on the K-W-L chart, but students generated the ideas and the questions.

Teachers introduce a K-W-L chart at the beginning of a unit and use it to identify what students already know about the topic and what they want to learn. Toward the end of the unit, students complete the last section of the chart, what they have learned. This instructional procedure helps students combine new information with prior knowledge and develop their vocabularies. It is intended to be used with nonfiction topics.

K	W	L
What We Know	**What We Want to Learn**	**What We Learned**
They hatch from eggs.	Are their feet called wabbly?	Chickens' bodies are covered with feathers.
They sleep.	Do they live in the woods?	Chickens have 4 claws.
They can be yellow or other colors.	What are their bodies covered with?	Yes, they do have stomachs.
They have 2 legs.	How many toes do they have?	Chickens like to play in the sun.
They have 2 wings.		
They eat food.	Do they have a stomach?	They like to stay warm.
They have a tail.	What noises do they make?	They live on farms.
They live on a farm.		
They are little.	Do they like the sun?	
They have beaks.		
They are covered with fluff.		

FIGURE 22–1   A Kindergarten Class's K-W-L Chart on Baby Chicks

STEP BY STEP

The steps in using a K-W-L chart are:

1. *Create a large chart.* As shown in Figure 22–1, teachers divide the chart into three columns and label them *K* (What We **K**now), *W* (What We **W**onder or What We **W**ant to Learn), and *L* (What We **L**earned).

2. *Complete the K column.* At the beginning of the thematic unit, teachers ask students to brainstorm what they know about the topic and write this information in the *K* (What We Know) column. Sometimes students suggest information that is not correct, and these statements should be turned into questions and added to the *W* (What We Wonder) column.

3. *Complete the W column.* Teachers write the questions that students suggest in the *W* column. They continue to add questions to the *W* column and begin to write information that students learn in the *L* (What We Learned) column.

4. *Complete the L column.* At the end of the unit, teachers complete the *L* column of the chart and have students reflect on what they have learned during the unit.

APPLICATIONS AND EXAMPLES

Older students can make K-W-L charts in pairs or small groups or make individual charts to organize and document their learning. Class charts, however, are more effective for younger children, and for older students who have not made K-W-L charts before. Students can make individual flip charts by folding a legal-size sheet of paper in half, lengthwise. Next, they cut the top flap into thirds and label them *K, W,* and *L.* Then students lift the flaps to write in each column, as shown in Figure 22–2.

REFERENCES

Ogle, D. M. (1986). K-W-L: A teaching model that develops active reading of expository text. *The Reading Teacher, 39,* 564–570.

Ogle, D. M. (1989). The know, want to know, learn strategy. In K. D. Muth (Ed.), *Children's comprehension of text: Research into practice* (pp. 205–223). Newark, DE: International Reading Association.

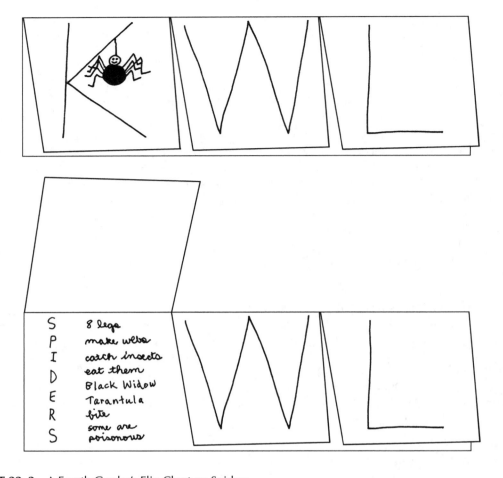

FIGURE 22–2 A Fourth Grader's Flip Chart on Spiders

23 Language Experience Approach

- ● literature focus units
- ○ literature circles
- ○ reading-writing workshop
- ● thematic units

- ● preK
- ● K–2
- ○ 3–5
- ○ 6–8

- ● individual
- ● pairs
- ● small group
- ● whole class

The language experience approach (LEA) is based on children's language and experiences (Ashton-Warner, 1965; Lee & Allen, 1963; Stauffer, 1970). In this approach, students dictate words and sentences about their experiences, and the teacher writes the dictation for them. As they write, teachers model how written language works. The text they develop becomes the reading material because it has been written with conventional English spelling. Because the language comes from the students themselves and because the content is based on their experiences, they are usually able to read the text easily. Reading and writing are connected as students are actively involved in reading what they have written.

The language experience approach is an effective way to help students emerge into reading. Even students who have not been successful with other types of reading activities can read what they have dictated. There is a drawback, however: Teachers provide a "perfect" model when they take students' dictation—they write neatly and spell words correctly. After language experience activities, some young children are not eager to do their own writing; they prefer their teacher's "perfect" writing to their own childlike writing. To avoid this problem, young children should be doing their own writing in journals and books, and participating in interactive writing activities at the same time they are participating in language experience activities so they will learn that sometimes they do their own writing and at other times the teacher takes their dictation.

STEP BY STEP

The steps in the language experience approach are:

1. *Provide an experience.* The experience serves as the stimulus for the writing. For group writing, it can be an experience shared in school, a book read aloud, a field trip, or some other experience that students are familiar with, such as having a pet or playing in the snow. For individual writing, the stimulus can be any experience that is important for the particular student.

2. *Talk about the experience.* The teacher and students talk about the experience to generate words and review the experience so that the students' dictation will be more interesting and complete. Teachers often begin with an open-ended question, such as "What are we going to write about?" As students talk about their experiences, they clarify and organize ideas, use more specific vocabulary, and extend their understanding.

3. *Record the student's dictation.* Texts for pairs or individual students are written on sheets of writing paper or in small booklets, and group texts are written on chart paper. Teachers print neatly and spell words correctly, but they preserve students' language as much as possible. It is a great temptation to change the student's language to the teacher's own, in either word choice or grammar, but editing should be kept to a minimum so that students do not get the impression that their language is inferior or inadequate.

 Teachers use the language experience approach to create reading materials that English learners can read and that interest them. Students cut pictures out of magazines and glue them in a book. Then the teacher and students identify and label several important words in the picture and create a sentence related to the picture. Then the teacher writes the sentence underneath the picture and the students reread it.

For individual texts, teachers continue to take the student's dictation and write until the student finishes or hesitates. If the student hesitates, the teacher rereads what has been written and encourages the student to continue. For group texts, students take turns dictating sentences, and after writing each sentence, the teacher rereads it.

4. *Read the text aloud, pointing to each word.* This reading reminds students of the content of the text and demonstrates how to read it aloud with appropriate intonation. Then students join in the reading. After reading group texts together, individual students can take turns rereading. Group texts can also be copied so each student has a copy to read independently.

5. *Extend the writing and reading experience.* Students might draw illustrations to accompany the text, or they can add this text to a collection of their writings to read and reread. Teachers often put a sheet of plastic over class charts so students can circle key words or other familiar words in the text. When they write individual texts, students can also read their texts to classmates from the author's chair. Students can take their own individual texts and copies of the class text home to share with family members.

6. *Make sentence strips.* Teachers rewrite the text on sentence strips or on small strips of tagboard that students keep in envelopes. They read and sequence the sentence strips, and after they can read the sentence strips smoothly, students cut the strips into individual words. Students arrange the words into the familiar sentence and then create new sentences with the word cards. Later the word cards are added to the student's word bank. Word banks can be made from small boxes, or holes can be punched in the word cards and they can be added to a word ring.

APPLICATIONS AND EXAMPLES

The language experience approach is often used to create texts students can read and use as a resource for writing in a thematic unit. For example, during a science unit on ladybugs in a first- and second-grade combination class, the teacher read aloud these stories, informational books, and poems: *Ladybug* (Watts, 1987), *The Grouchy Ladybug* (Carle, 1986), *Ladybug, Ladybug* (Brown, 1988), and *The Ladybug and Other Insects* (Goldsen, 1989). With this knowledge about ladybugs, students dictated this text:

Part 1: What Ladybugs Do

Ladybugs are helper insects. They help people because they eat aphids. They make the earth pretty. They are red and they have 7 black spots. Ladybugs keep their wings under the red wing cases. Their wings are transparent and they fly with these wings. Ladybugs love to eat aphids. They love them so much that they can eat 50 aphids in one day!

Part 2: How Ladybugs Grow

Ladybugs live on leaves in bushes and in tree trunks. They lay eggs that are sticky and yellow on a leaf. The eggs hatch and out come tiny and black larvae. They like to eat aphids, too. Next the larva becomes a pupa and then it changes into a ladybug. When the ladybugs first come out of the pupa, they are yellow but they change into red and their spots appear. Then they can fly.

Part 3: Ladybugs Are Smart

Ladybugs have a good trick so that the birds won't eat them. If a bird starts to attack, the ladybug turns over on her back and squeezes a stinky liquid from her legs. It smells terrible and makes the bird fly away.

Each part was written on a separate sheet of chart paper. Next, the students each chose a sentence to be written on a sentence strip. Some students wrote their own sentence, and the teacher wrote sentences for other students. They practiced reading their sentences and read them to classmates. Then they cut the sentences apart and rearranged them. Later, students used the sentences in class collaborations and individual "All About Ladybugs" books. Figure 23–1 shows how students used the words in the dictated text to read and write.

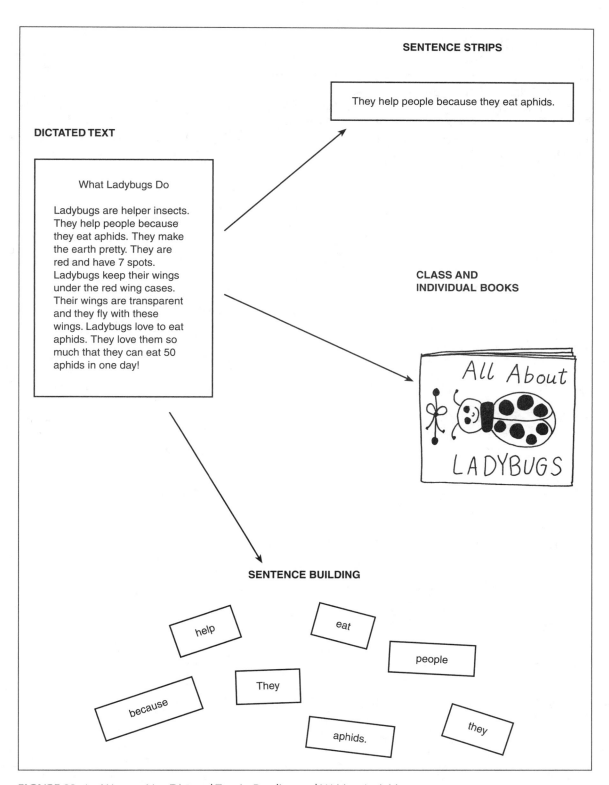

SENTENCE STRIPS

They help people because they eat aphids.

DICTATED TEXT

What Ladybugs Do

Ladybugs are helper insects. They help people because they eat aphids. They make the earth pretty. They are red and have 7 spots. Ladybugs keep their wings under the red wing cases. Their wings are transparent and they fly with these wings. Ladybugs love to eat aphids. They love them so much that they can eat 50 aphids in one day!

CLASS AND INDIVIDUAL BOOKS

All About LADYBUGS

SENTENCE BUILDING

help

eat

people

They

because

aphids.

they

FIGURE 23–1 Ways to Use Dictated Text in Reading and Writing Activities

REFERENCES

Ashton-Warner, S. (1965). *Teacher*. New York: Simon & Schuster.

Brown, R. (1988). *Ladybug, ladybug*. New York: Dutton.

Carle, E. (1986). *The grouchy ladybug*. New York: Harper & Row.

Goldsen, L. (1989). *The ladybug and other insects*. New York: Scholastic.

Lee, D. M., & Allen, R. V. (1963). *Learning to read through experience* (2nd ed.). New York: Meredith.

Stauffer, R. G. (1970). *Directing the reading-thinking process*. New York: Harper & Row.

Watts, B. (1987). *Ladybug*. Morristown, NJ: Silver Burdett.

24 Learning Logs

○ literature focus units	○ preK	● individual
○ literature circles	● K–2	○ pairs
○ reading-writing workshop	● 3–5	○ small group
● thematic units	● 6–8	○ whole class

Students write in learning logs as part of across-the-curriculum thematic units. Learning logs, like other types of journals, are notebooks or booklets of paper in which students record information they are learning, write questions and reflections about their learning, and make charts, diagrams, and clusters (Bromley, 1993; Tompkins, 2004). The great value of learning logs is that students use them as tools for learning.

 ## STEP BY STEP

The steps in making a learning log are:

1. *Prepare learning logs.* At the beginning of a thematic unit, students make learning logs using lined or unlined paper and tagboard, laminated construction paper, or wallpaper covers.
2. *Plan activities for students to use their learning logs.* Examples include taking notes, drawing diagrams, quickwriting, and clustering. Students' writing is impromptu in learning logs, and the emphasis is on using writing as a learning tool rather than creating polished products. Even so, students should be encouraged to work carefully and to spell content-related words posted on the word wall correctly.
3. *Monitor students' entries.* Teachers read students' learning logs and answer their questions and clarify confusions.

 ## APPLICATIONS AND EXAMPLES

Students use learning logs during social studies units to make notes and respond to information they are learning as they read informational books and content-area textbooks. They also make data charts, clusters, maps, time lines, and other charts in learning logs. During a thematic unit on pioneers, for example, students do these activities in learning logs:

- Write questions to investigate during the unit
- Draw pictures of covered wagons
- List items the pioneers carried west
- Mark the Oregon Trail on a map of the United States
- Make clusters of information read in books
- Write responses to videos about pioneers
- Write a rough draft of a poem about life on the Oregon Trail
- Write a letter to the teacher at the end of the unit listing the five most important things they learned

Learning logs are used for similar purposes in science units. During a unit on rocks and minerals, for example, seventh graders made clusters that they completed as they read a chapter in the science text-book, compiled lab reports as they did experiments, did quickwrites after watching videos, and drew

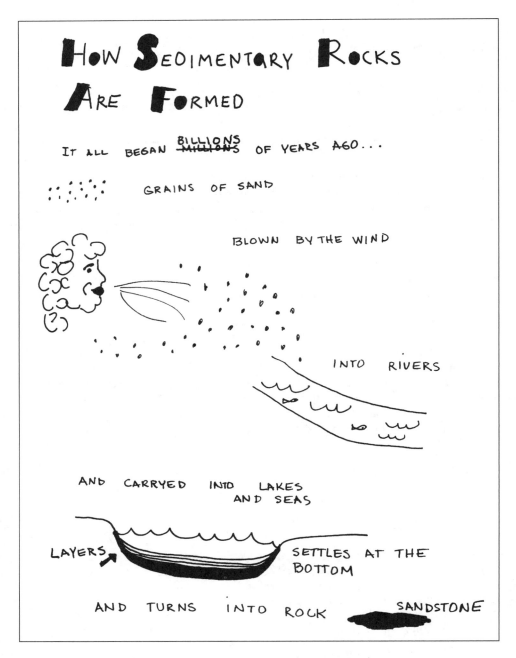

FIGURE 24–1   Seventh Graders' Learning Log Entries on Sedimentary Rocks

diagrams and charts about scientific information. Students made the two entries shown in Figure 24–1. In one entry, a student used a series of illustrations to explain how sedimentary rocks are formed; in the other, a student charted the four types of sedimentary rocks.

Students also use learning logs to write about what they are learning in math. They record explanations and examples of concepts presented in class, write story problems, and react to mathematical concepts they are learning and any problems they may be having. For example, during a unit on money, students draw pictures of coins and bills, make a data chart showing the combinations of coins to equal $1.00, write story problems using cents-off coupons and advertisements cut out of the newspaper, and

FIGURE 24–1 *continued*

write quickwrites about how they spend and save money. Some upper-grade teachers allow students the last 5 minutes of math class to summarize the day's lesson and react to it in their learning logs.

REFERENCES

Bromley, K. (1993). *Journaling: Engagements in reading, writing, and thinking.* New York: Scholastic.
Tompkins, G. E. (2004). *Teaching writing: Balancing process and product* (4th ed.). Upper Saddle River, NJ: Merrill/Prentice Hall.

25

Literacy Centers

● literature focus units	● preK	○ individual
○ literature circles	○ K–2	○ pairs
○ reading-writing workshop	● 3–5	● small group
○ thematic units	● 6–8	○ whole class

Literacy centers contain meaningful, purposeful literacy activities that students can work at in small groups. They are usually organized in special places in the classroom or at groups of tables (Fountas & Pinnell, 1996). A variety of literacy centers, including word making, library, skills, publishing, computers, and puppets, can be used during literature focus units. Descriptions of 20 centers used in elementary classrooms are given in Figure 25–1. Centers are usually associated with primary classrooms,

Author	Information about an author that students are studying is displayed in this center. Often posters, books, and videotapes about the author are available for students to examine, and students may also write letters to the author at this center.
Class Collaborations	Students write pages to be added to a class book at this center. Each student contributes a page according to guidelines established before students visit this center. Afterwards, the teacher compiles and binds the book.
Computer	A bank of computers with word processing and drawing programs, interactive books on CD-ROM, and other computer programs are available at the center.
Data Charts	As part of social studies and science units, students compile information for data charts. Students consult informational books and reference books at the center and add information to a large class data chart or to individual data charts.
Dramatic Play	Literacy materials and environmental print are added to play centers so that students can learn about authentic purposes for reading and writing. Food packages, for example, are placed in housekeeping centers, and street signs are added to block centers.
Library	A wide variety of books and other reading materials, organized according to topic or reading level, are available in classroom libraries. Students choose books at their reading level to read and reread.
Listening	Students use a tape player and headphones to listen to stories and other texts read aloud. Often copies of the texts are available so that students can read along as they listen.
Making Words	Letter cards, magnetic letters, and white boards that students use to spell and write words are available in this center. Students often create specific words that follow a spelling pattern or sort letters to spell a variety of two-, three-, four-, and five-letter words.
Message	Mailboxes or a bulletin board is set up in the message center so that students can write notes and send them to classmates. Also included in the center are a list of names, stickers to use as stamps, postcards, and a variety of writing paper and envelopes.
Phonics	A variety of small objects, picture cards, magnetic letters, letter cards, and small white boards are used in this center. Students practice phonics concepts that teachers have already taught, such as matching rhyming word pictures, sorting a box of objects according to the beginning sound or vowel sound that the name of the object represents, or writing a series of words representing a word family such as *-ill.*

FIGURE 25–1 Twenty Literacy Centers

Pocket Charts	Teachers set out sentence strips or word cards for a familiar song or poem, and students arrange the sentence strips or words in the pocket chart so that they can read the poem or sing the song. Students often have extra sentence strips and word cards so that they can create new versions and write variations.
Poetry	Charts describing various poetic forms are available in this center, and students write formula poems there. They often use poetic forms that teachers have already introduced to the class.
Proofreading	Students use spellcheckers, word walls of high-frequency words, and dictionaries to proofread compositions they have written. Students often work with partners at this center.
Puppets	Puppets and puppet stages and small manipulative materials related to books students are reading are set out for students to use in this center. Students use the materials to retell stories and create sequels to stories.
Reading and Writing the Classroom	This center is stocked with reading wands (wooden dowel rods with eraser tips) and glasses (with the lenses removed) for students to use as they walk around the classroom and point at and read words, sentences, and books. Also included are small clipboards and pens that students use as they walk around the classroom and record familiar words and sentences posted there.
Sequencing	Students sequence sets of pictures about the events in a story or story boards (made by cutting apart two copies of a picture book and backing each page with poster board). Students can also make story boards for picture books and chapter books at this center.
Skills	Students practice skills teachers have taught in minilessons at this center. Teachers place the materials they used in the minilesson in the center for students to use. Students sort word cards, write additional examples on charts, and manipulate other materials.
Spelling	Students use white boards and magnetic letters to practice spelling words.
Word Sorts	Students sort word cards into categories according to meaning or structural forms. Sometimes students paste the sorted words on sheets of poster board, and at other times, they sort the words as a practice activity but do not paste them into categories.
Writing	This center is stocked with writing materials, including pens, papers, blank books, postcards, dictionaries, and word walls, that students use for a variety of writing activities. Bookmaking supplies such as cardboard, wallpaper, cloth, paper, wide-arm staplers, yarn, brads, and marking pens are also available.

FIGURE 25–1   *continued*

but they can be used effectively at all grade levels. In some classrooms, all students work at centers at the same time, whereas in other classrooms, most of the students work in centers while the teacher works with other small groups of students.

The activities in these centers relate to stories students are reading in literature focus groups and to skills and strategies recently presented in minilessons. Students often manipulate objects, sort word cards, reread books, write responses to stories, and practice skills in the centers. They rarely, if ever, do worksheets at the centers. Some centers, such as writing and library centers, are often permanent centers, but other centers change according to the teacher's goals.

In some classrooms, students flow freely from center to center according to their interests; in other classrooms, students are assigned to centers or required to work at some "assigned" centers and choose among other "choice" centers. Students can sign attendance sheets when they work at each center or mark off their names on a class list tacked to each center. Rarely do students move from center to center in a lockstep approach every 15 to 30 minutes; instead, they move to another center when they finish what they are doing at one center.

STEP BY STEP

The steps in using literacy centers are:

1. *Set up the centers.* Teachers organize 4 to 10 centers, each with directions, supplies, and space to accommodate a small group of students. They explain and demonstrate to students the types of activities involved in each center.
2. *Have students move into centers to work.* The teacher circulates and provides guidance on how to work at the centers and how to do the activities there.
3. *Use a management system.* Teachers have students keep track of their work in the centers using sign-in sheets, clothespins clipped to a chart, or another management system.
4. *Monitor students' progress.* Teachers monitor students as they move from center to center, and reinforce guidelines for completing assignments.
5. *Modify centers.* Teachers modify centers as necessary to keep students' interest, provide opportunities to practice skills being taught, and extend students' learning about the featured book in the literature focus unit.

APPLICATIONS AND EXAMPLES

Literacy centers are used in a variety of ways. In a first-grade classroom, for example, during a literature focus unit on *If You Give a Mouse a Cookie* (Numeroff, 1985), students might work at these centers:

- *Writing Center.* Students write books about their favorite cookies or write their own versions of Numeroff's story.
- *Phonics Center.* Students sort objects and put those that end with /s/ (as in *mouse*) into one bucket and all other objects into another bucket. Or they might sort a group of objects from the story (napkin, cookie, straw, comb) into two buckets according to the number of syllables in the word.
- *Listening Center.* Students listen to audiotapes of *If You Give a Mouse a Cookie* or *If You Give a Moose a Muffin* (Numeroff, 1991).
- *Observation Center.* Students observe two mice in a cage and draw pictures and write observations in their reading logs.
- *Sequencing Center.* Students retell the story and arrange a set of pictures representing events in the story into a circle.
- *Making Words Center.* Students use magnetic letters to write *mouse, cookie,* and other words from the story.

In a seventh-grade classroom, students reading *Catherine, Called Birdy* (Cushman, 1994), a story set in the Middle Ages, participate in these centers:

- *Writing Center.* Students write in the double-entry journals.
- *Class Collaboration Center.* Students create pages for the class alphabet book on the Middle Ages.
- *Library Center.* Students read other books about the Middle Ages.
- *Word Wall Center.* Students add words related to the Middle Ages, such as *tournaments* and *dowry,* to their word wall. They check the dictionary definition of the word and draw a picture to describe or define the word.

- *Skills Center.* Students work with partners to create open-mind portraits of Birdy at several key points in the story.
- *Poetry Center.* Students work in small groups to create found poems using phrases from the story. They write their poems on the computer.
- *Making Words Center.* Students rearrange letter cards that spell the title of the book to spell as many words as they can. They list the words they create on chart paper according to the number of letters in each word.

REFERENCES

Cushman, K. (1994). *Catherine, called Birdy.* New York: HarperCollins.

Fountas, I. C., & Pinnell, G. S. (1996). *Guided reading: Good first teaching for all children.* Portsmouth, NH: Heinemann.

Numeroff, L. (1985). *If you give a mouse a cookie.* New York: HarperCollins.

Numeroff, L. (1991). *If you give a moose a muffin.* New York: HarperCollins.

26 Making Words

● literature focus units	○ preK	● individual
○ literature circles	● K–2	● pairs
○ reading-writing workshop	● 3–5	● small group
○ thematic units	○ 6–8	● whole class

Making words is an activity in which students arrange letter cards to spell words. As they make words using letter cards, they practice phonics and spelling concepts (Cunningham & Cunningham, 1992; Gunning, 1995). Teachers choose key words from books students are reading that exemplify particular phonics or spelling patterns for students to practice. Then they prepare a set of letter cards that small groups of students or individual students can use to spell words. The teacher leads students as they create a variety of words using the letters. For example, after reading *The Very Busy Spider* (Carle, 1984), a group of first graders built these short *i* and long *i* words using the letters in the word *spider: is, sip, rip, dip, drip, side, ride,* and *ripe.* After spelling these words, students used all of the letters to spell the key word—*spider.*

STEP BY STEP

The steps in a making words activity are:

1. *Make letter cards.* Teachers prepare a set of small letter cards (1- to 2-inch square cards) for students to use in word-making activities. For high-frequency letters (vowels, *s, t,* and *r*) they make three or four times as many letter cards as there are students in the class. For less frequently used letters, teachers make one or two times as many letter cards as there are students in the class. They print the lowercase letter form on one side of the letter cards and the uppercase form on the other side. They package cards with each letter separately in small boxes, plastic trays, or plastic bags. Teachers may also want to make a set of larger letter cards (3- to 6-inch square cards) to display in a pocket chart or on a chalk tray during the activity.

2. *Choose a word for the activity.* Teachers choose a word or spelling pattern to use in the word-making activity and have a student distribute the needed letter cards to individual students or to small groups of students.

3. *Name the letter cards.* Teachers ask students to name the letter cards and arrange them on one side of their desks.

4. *Make words using the cards.* Students use the letter cards to spell a particular word or words containing two, three, four, five, six, or more letters or using a particular spelling pattern. For example, students might use letter cards (*a, d, g, i, n, n, o, s, t, t, u*) to spell these three-letter words: *sit, tan, out, not, and, dog.* Then students use the same letter cards to spell four-letter words (e.g., *sing, nuts, said*), five-letter words (e.g., *stand, doing, giant*), and longer words until they use all of the letters to spell *outstanding.* Or, with a different set of cards, students might spell *at* and then add a beginning letter to spell *cat, hat,* or another rhyming word. With other letter cards, students might spell *rid* and *fed* and then change the words to *ride* and *feed* to practice ways to spell long-vowel sounds. The teacher monitors students' spellings and encourages them to fix any misspelled words. As students spell the words, a student or the teacher can arrange the large letter cards to spell the same words or record the spellings on chart paper or on the chalkboard.

5. *Share word cards.* Teachers show word cards with some of the words that students have made. They ask students to read the words and place them in a pocket chart or on the chalk tray. After reading all of the words, teachers point out particular spelling patterns and group the word cards according to the patterns.

APPLICATIONS AND EXAMPLES

Teachers choose words for word-making lessons from books they are reading with students. For example, after reading Sue Williams's *I Went Walking* (1989), *walking* is a good choice for word-making activities; after reading Eric Carle's *A House for Hermit Crab* (1987), *hermit crabs* offers many word-making possibilities; and after reading Laura Numeroff's *Chimps Don't Wear Glasses* (1995), *chimpanzee* works well. Upper-grade teachers also choose words and phrases from chapter books they are reading for word-making activities. After reading *Number the Stars* (Lowry, 1989), *resistance fighters* can be used, and after reading *Tuck Everlasting* (Babbitt, 1975), the title works well. Teachers can also identify other words that work well for word-making activities using two books that Patricia Cunningham and Dorothy Hall have compiled (1994a, 1994b).

A third-grade teacher passed out the letters cards to spell *feather* after reading *Don't Fidget a Feather!* (Silverman, 1994), but she didn't tell students what the letters spelled. First she asked students to make all of the two-letter words that they could. They spelled *he* and *at,* and she wrote the words on a chart. Then she asked them to make three-letter words, and they spelled *are, eat, art, fat, rat, hat, the, ate,* and *her;* she added these words to the chart. Then she asked students to spell *ear* and to substitute beginning sounds to spell *hear, fear,* and *tear.* Next she asked students for another way to spell *hear* and they spelled *here.* Then she asked them to add a letter to spell *heart.* The students noticed that *heart* is made of two small words, *he* and *art.* The teacher also added all of these words to the chart, as shown in Figure 26–1. Finally, students spelled *father,* using all of the letters except one of the *e*'s, and then she asked students to find a way to add the remaining *e;* they spelled *feather* and commented that the *ea* spelling represents a short *e* sound. After the whole-class activity, the teacher placed a set of letter

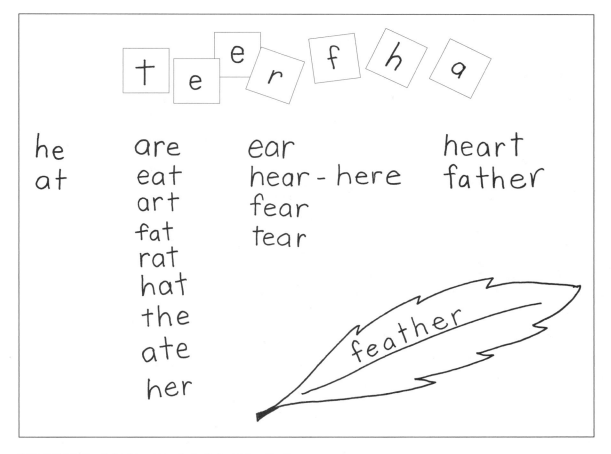

FIGURE 26–1   A Making Words Activity Using *Feather*

cards in a literacy center so that students could practice making words with the letters in *feather* and refer to the chart she made whenever necessary.

REFERENCES

Babbitt, N. (1975). *Tuck everlasting.* New York: Farrar, Straus & Giroux.

Carle, E. (1984). *The very busy spider.* New York: Philomel.

Carle, E. (1987). *A house for hermit crab.* Saxonville, MA: Picture Book Studio.

Cunningham, P. M., & Cunningham, J. W. (1992). Making words: Enhancing the invented spelling-decoding connection. *The Reading Teacher, 46,* 106–115.

Cunningham, P. M., & Hall, D. P. (1994a). *Making big words.* Parsippany, NJ: Good Apple.

Cunningham, P. M., & Hall, D. P. (1994b). *Making words.* Parsippany, NJ: Good Apple.

Gunning, T. G. (1995). Word building: A strategic approach to the teaching of phonics. *The Reading Teacher, 48,* 484–488.

Lowry, L. (1989). *Number the stars.* Boston: Houghton Mifflin.

Numeroff, L. (1995). *Chimps don't wear glasses.* New York: Simon & Schuster.

Silverman, E. (1994). *Don't fidget a feather!* New York: Simon & Schuster.

Williams, S. (1989). *I went walking.* San Diego: Harcourt Brace Jovanovich.

27 Minilessons

- literature focus units
- literature circles
- reading-writing workshop
- thematic units

- preK
- K–2
- 3–5
- 6–8

- ○ individual
- ○ pairs
- small group
- whole class

Teachers teach focused lessons called minilessons on literacy procedures, concepts, strategies, and skills (Atwell, 1987; Calkins, 1994). Examples of literacy procedures include how to make a puppet or how to write an entry in a reading log, and literacy concepts include sharing information about an author or teaching about homophones. Examples of skills are using commas in a series and using an index to locate information in a nonfiction book; examples of strategies are visualizing, making connections to one's own life during reading, and making a cluster before writing. In these lessons, teachers introduce or review a topic and connect the topic to the reading or writing students are involved in. Minilessons usually last 15 to 30 minutes, and sometimes teachers extend the lesson over several days as students explore the topic or apply it in their reading and writing activities. Teachers present minilessons to the whole class or to small groups, depending on students' needs. The best time to teach a minilesson is when students will have immediate opportunities to apply what they are learning.

STEP BY STEP

The steps in conducting a minilesson are:

1. *Introduce the procedure, concept, strategy, or skill.* Teachers share examples using books students are reading or students' own writing projects.

2. *Share examples of the topic.* Teachers demonstrate the topic or provide information and additional examples about the topic, making connections to students' reading or writing.

3. *Provide opportunities for practice.* Teachers involve students in opportunities to practice the procedure, concept, strategy, or skill. Through practice activities, students bring together the information and examples presented earlier.

4. *Have students take notes.* Students make notes about the topic on a poster to be displayed in the classroom or in language arts notebooks.

5. *Have students reflect.* Students consider how they can apply this information in their reading and writing. Then provide additional opportunities for students to use the procedure, concept, strategy, or skill they are learning in meaningful ways.

APPLICATIONS AND EXAMPLES

Teachers teach minilessons on a wide variety of literacy procedures, concepts, skills, and strategies. Figure 27–1 shows how teachers use the five steps to teach three minilessons. The first example is a minilesson to teach second graders about the *-ing* inflectional ending; the second teaches fourth graders how to make open-mind portraits of characters; and the third minilesson is a review of homophones for sixth graders.

	-ing Inflectional Ending	Open-Mind Portraits	Homophones
1. *Introduction*	Introduce *-ing* as an inflectional ending and have students "read the classroom" to locate examples of words with *-ing* endings. Have students write these words on a chart.	Introduce open-mind portraits as an activity to help students think more deeply about a character in a book they are reading, and show a sample open-mind portrait of a character from a book that students have read.	Review homophones. Explain that homophones are words that sound alike but are spelled differently. Use *there–their–they're* and *pair–pear* as examples.
2. *Examples*	Reread the word chart with students and add more words from books students are reading. Have students circle the root or main word in each word. Explain that the final consonant in short-vowel words (e.g., *swim*) is doubled before adding the ending.	Demonstrate how to make an open-mind portrait for a character in a book students are reading.	Have students brainstorm a list of homophones, particularly those that confuse them. Also, encourage students to share their mnemonic devices for remembering when to use each word.
3. *Practice*	Have students practice locating, reading, and writing *-ing* words in literacy centers. Students locate *-ing* words on interactive charts, form *-ing* words with magnetic letters, and write *-ing* words on dry-erase boards.	Review the steps in the procedure, and have students each make an open-mind portrait of the same character or a different character in the book they are reading.	Have students review their rough drafts that have been edited to locate the homophone errors that they make. Have students compile a list of those that they make most often.
4. *Note making*	Have students write little books of *-ing* words and draw circles around the root words.	Have students participate in making a class chart on the steps in making an open-mind portrait that they can refer to when making other portraits. Use interactive writing to write the chart.	Have students each make a chart that they can use to avoid making homophone errors when they write.
5. *Reflection*	After several days, have students reread books they have written recently and locate *-ing* words they have written.	Have students share their open-mind portraits with classmates and talk about how this activity helped them to think more deeply about the characters in the book they were reading.	After a week or two, have students check their writing for homophone errors and then quickwrite to reflect on whether or not they are continuing to make homophone errors.

FIGURE 27–1   Steps in Teaching Three Minilessons

REFERENCES

Atwell, N. (1987). *In the middle: Writing, reading, and thinking with adolescents.* Portsmouth, NH: Heinemann/Boynton/Cook.

Calkins, L. M. (1994). *The art of teaching writing* (2nd ed.). Portsmouth, NH: Heinemann.

28 Open-Mind Portraits

- ● literature focus units
- ● literature circles
- ○ reading-writing workshop
- ○ thematic units

- ○ preK
- ○ K–2
- ● 3–5
- ● 6–8

- ● individual
- ● pairs
- ○ small group
- ○ whole class

To help students think more deeply about a character and reflect on story events from the character's viewpoint, students draw an open-mind portrait of the character. These portraits have two parts: the face of the character on the top page, and the mind of the character on the second page (Tompkins, 2003). Sometimes students add several "mind" pages to show a character's mind at pivotal points in a story. As students draw open-mind portraits, they are visually representing the character and his or her thoughts.

The two pages of a fourth grader's open-mind portrait on Sarah, the mail-order bride in *Sarah, Plain and Tall* (MacLachlan, 1983), is shown in Figure 28–1. The words and pictures on her "mind" page represent her thinking at the end of the story.

FIGURE 28–1 A Fourth Grader's Open-Mind Portrait of Sarah, the Main Character of *Sarah, Plain and Tall*

STEP BY STEP

The steps in making an open-mind portrait are:

1. *Make a portrait of a character.* Students draw and color a portrait of the head and neck of a character in a book they are reading.
2. *Cut out the portrait and open-mind pages.* Students cut out the portrait and attach it with a brad or staple on top of another sheet of drawing paper. It is important that students place the brad or staple at the top of the portrait.
3. *Design the mind pages.* Students lift the portrait and draw and write about the character's thoughts on the second page. They can add several extra sheets to show the character's thoughts at key points in the story.
4. *Share the completed open-mind portraits.* Students share their portraits with classmates and talk about the words and pictures they chose to include in the mind of the character.

APPLICATIONS AND EXAMPLES

Students create open-mind portraits to think more deeply about a character in a story they are reading. They often reread parts of the story to recall specific details about the character's appearance before they draw the portrait, and they write several entries in a simulated journal to start thinking from that character's viewpoint before making the second page of the open-mind portrait. In addition to making open-mind portraits of characters in stories they are reading, students can make open-mind portraits of historical figures as part of social studies units, and of well-known personalities after reading their biographies.

REFERENCES

MacLachlan, P. (1983). *Sarah, plain and tall.* New York: HarperCollins.
Tompkins, G. E. (2003). *Literacy for the 21st century* (3rd ed.). Upper Saddle River, NJ: Merrill/Prentice Hall.

29

Plot Profiles

- ● literature focus units
- ● literature circles
- ○ reading-writing workshop
- ○ thematic units

- ○ preK
- ○ K–2
- ● 3–5
- ● 6–8

- ○ individual
- ● pairs
- ● small group
- ● whole class

Students make plot profiles to examine the plot of a novel or chapter book story. After reading each chapter, students mark a graph to track the tension or excitement of the story (Johnson & Louis, 1987). Figure 29–1 presents a plot profile for *Stone Fox* (Gardiner, 1980), a story about a boy who wins a dogsled race to save his grandfather's farm. Fourth graders met in small groups to talk about each chapter, and after these discussions, the whole class came together to decide how to mark the graph. At the end of the story, students analyzed the chart and rationalized that the tension dips in Chapters 3 and 7 because the story would be too stressful without these dips.

Teachers often introduce plot profiles as they teach students about the plot development of a story (Tompkins, 2002). Students learn that plot is the sequence of events involving characters in conflict situations and that a story's plot is based on the goals of one or more characters and how they go about attaining these goals. Chapter by chapter, as they read and mark a plot profile, students talk about plot development and the conflict situations in which characters are involved. They also learn that conflict is the tension between the forces in the plot and that it is what interests readers enough to continue reading the story. They find examples of the different types of conflict—conflict between a character and nature, between a character and society, between characters, or within a character—in the stories they read (Lukens, 1995).

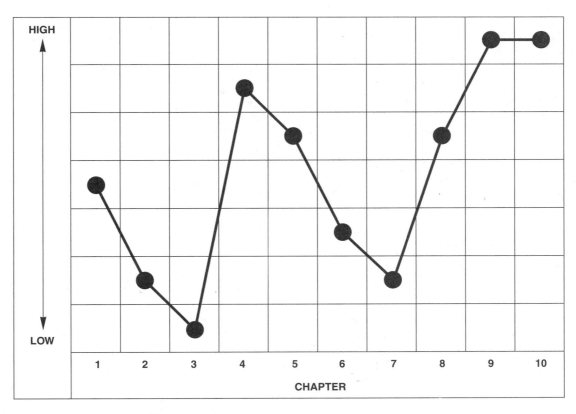

FIGURE 29–1 A Plot Profile for *Stone Fox*

Plot profiles also help students comprehend complex stories. By asking students to think about the conflict and tension in the story, teachers draw their attention back to this basic structure of the story. Students read each chapter with a purpose in mind—understanding the conflict or tension in the story. Then, as they talk about the story, students ask questions and offer comments, their classmates clarify misconceptions and offer comments, and all students' understanding of the story grows. At the end of the book, the plot profile provides a visual representation for students to use in deepening their comprehension of the story.

STEP BY STEP

The steps in making a plot profile are:

1. *Prepare the plot profile chart.* Teachers draw a large plot profile chart with a column for each chapter and five to seven rows for the tension range on chart paper or butcher paper to display in the classroom. They also make small, individual copies of the plot profile for each child.

2. *Introduce the chart.* Teachers and students read and discuss the first chapter of the book. The discussion should focus on the plot development of the story and the tension in the chapter. Teachers may want to have students begin by discussing the chapter in small groups and then come together as a class to finish the discussion. Then teachers introduce the plot profile chart and explain that they will make a graph on the chart to examine how the author developed the plot. Together the class decides on the level of tension in the first chapter and how they will mark the chart. One student marks the class chart and all students mark their individual charts.

3. *Have students continue graphing the plot.* Students continue to read, discuss, and mark the tension of each chapter on the plot profile chart. The chart can be made as a line graph or a bar graph.

4. *Reflect on the chart.* After students finish reading the story and marking the tension on the chart, they have a grand conversation to discuss how the author developed the plot of the story. Teachers encourage students to think about the impact of the conflict and story events on the characters. Students write a reflection about the plot development of the story in their reading logs, or they write an essay to accompany their completed plot profiles.

APPLICATIONS AND EXAMPLES

Plot profiles are designed for chapter book stories, not picture book stories, because picture books are shorter and usually are not separated into sections as chapter books are. Chapter books in which main characters struggle to overcome great odds, or books in which there is a great deal of conflict, such as *Hatchet* (Paulsen, 1987), *The Giver* (Lowry, 1993), and *Shiloh* (Naylor, 1991), work well for plot profiles.

REFERENCES

Gardiner, J. R. (1980). *Stone Fox.* New York: Harper & Row.

Johnson, T. D., & Louis, D. R. (1987). *Literacy through literature.* Portsmouth, NH: Heinemann.

Lowry, L. (1993). *The giver.* Boston: Houghton Mifflin.

Lukens, R. J. (1995). *A critical handbook of children's literature* (5th ed.). New York: HarperCollins.

Naylor, P. R. (1991). *Shiloh.* New York: Atheneum.

Paulsen, G. (1987). *Hatchet.* New York: Bradbury.

Tompkins, G. E. (2002). *Language arts: Content and teaching strategies* (5th ed.). Upper Saddle River, NJ: Merrill/Prentice Hall.

30 Prereading Plans

○ literature focus units   ○ preK   ○ individual
○ literature circles   ○ K–2   ○ pairs
○ reading-writing workshop   ● 3–5   ○ small group
● thematic units   ● 6–8   ● whole class

Teachers use a prereading plan (PReP) to diagnose students' prior knowledge and build necessary background knowledge before students read informational books and content-area textbooks (Langer, 1981; Tierney, Readence, & Dishner, 1995). Teachers introduce a key concept discussed in the reading assignment and ask students to brainstorm related words and ideas. Teachers and students talk about the concept, and afterwards students quickwrite or quickdraw to reflect on it. With this prereading preparation, students are better able to comprehend the reading assignment. This activity is especially important when students have limited background knowledge about a topic or technical vocabulary, as well as for students who are learning English as a second language.

STEP BY STEP

The steps using a prereading plan are:

1. *Discuss a key concept.* Teachers introduce a key concept to students by using a word, phrase, object, or picture to initiate a discussion.
2. *Brainstorm.* Teachers ask students to brainstorm words about the topic and record their ideas on a chart. They also help students make connections among the brainstormed ideas.
3. *Introduce vocabulary.* Teachers present additional vocabulary words that students need to read the assignment and clarify any misconceptions.
4. *Quickwrite about the topic.* Teachers have students draw pictures and/or quickwrite about the topic using words from the brainstormed list.
5. *Share the quickwrites.* Students share their quickwrites with the class, and teachers ask questions to help students clarify and elaborate their work.
6. *Read the assignment.* Students read the assignment and relate what they are reading to what they learned before reading.

APPLICATIONS AND EXAMPLES

Before reading a social studies textbook chapter about the Bill of Rights, an eighth-grade teacher used PReP to introduce the concept that citizens have freedoms and responsibilities. Students brainstormed this list during a discussion of the Bill of Rights:

guaranteed in the Constitution
James Madison
1791
10 amendments
citizens
freedom of speech

freedom of religion

freedom to assemble

homes can't be searched without a search warrant

owning guns and pistols

limits on these freedoms for everyone's good

"life, liberty, and the pursuit of happiness"

act responsibly

vote intelligently

right to a jury trial

serve on juries

no cruel or unusual punishments

death penalty

power to the people

serve in public offices—city council, school board, legislature, president

Then students wrote quickwrites to make personal connections to the ideas they brainstormed before reading the chapter. Here is one student's quickwrite:

> *I always knew America was a free country but I thought it was because of the Declaration of Independence. Now I know that the Bill of Rights is a list of our freedoms. There are ten freedoms in the Bill of Rights. I have the freedom to go to any church I want, to own guns, to speak my mind, and to have newspapers. I never thought of serving on a jury as a freedom and my Mom didn't either. She was on a jury about a year ago and she didn't want to do it. It took a whole week and her boss didn't like her missing work. The trial was about someone who robbed a store and shot a man but he didn't die. I'm going to tell her that it is important to do jury duty. When I am an adult, I hope I get to be on a jury of a murder trial. I want to protect my freedoms and I know it is a citizen's responsibility, too.*

When the teacher read this student's quickwrite, she identified several concepts that the class had discussed and noticed that the student confused the number of amendments with the number of freedoms listed in the amendments. The teacher clarified some misunderstandings individually with students and mentioned others during class discussions.

REFERENCES

Langer, J. A. (1981). From theory to practice: A prereading plan. *Journal of Reading, 25,* 152–157.

Tierney, R. J., Readence, J. E., & Dishner, E. K. (1995). *Reading strategies and practices: A compendium* (4th ed.). Boston: Allyn & Bacon.

Question-Answer-Relationships (QAR)

● literature focus units	○ preK	● individual
● literature circles	○ K–2	● pairs
○ reading-writing workshop	● 3–5	● small groups
● thematic units	● 6–8	● whole class

Taffy Raphael's question-answer-relationships (QAR) technique (Raphael & McKinney, 1983; Raphael & Wonnacott, 1985) teaches students to be consciously aware of whether they are likely to find the answer to a comprehension question "right there" on the page, between the lines, or beyond the information provided in the text. By being aware of the requirements posed by a question, students are in a better position to be able to answer it.

QAR differentiates among four types of questions and the kinds of thinking required to answer them. Some questions require only literal thinking whereas others demand higher inferential, application, or evaluation levels of thinking. The four types of questions are:

1. *Right There Questions.* Readers find the answer "right there" in the text, usually in the same sentence as words from the question. These are literal-level questions.

2. *Think and Search Questions.* The answer is in the text, but readers must search for it in different parts of the text and put the ideas together. These are inferential-level questions.

3. *Author and Me Questions.* Readers use a combination of the author's ideas and their own ideas to answer the question. These questions combine inferential and application levels.

4. *On My Own Questions.* Readers use their own ideas to answer the question; sometimes it is not even necessary to read the text to answer the question. These are application- and evaluation-level questions.

An eighth grader's chart describing these four types of questions is shown in Figure 31-1.

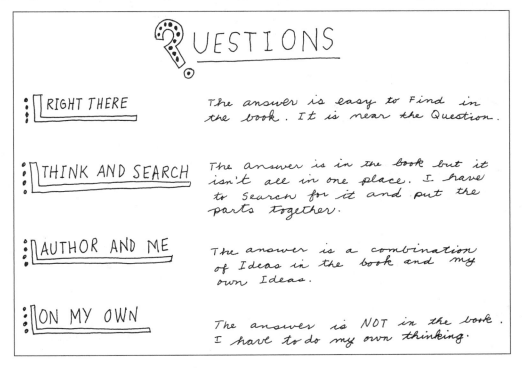

FIGURE 31–1 An Eighth Grader's QAR Chart

The first two types of questions are known as "in the book" questions because the answers to the questions can be found in the book, and the last two types of questions are "in the head" (Raphael, 1986) questions because they require information and ideas not presented in the book.

The goal of this strategy is for students to become more aware of the strategic nature of comprehension. After practicing the strategy, students should be encouraged to use it when they are reading both narrative and expository texts and when answering comprehension questions independently.

STEP BY STEP

The steps in the QAR strategy are:

1. *Read the questions before reading the text.* Students read the questions as a preview before reading the text to give them an idea of what to think about as they are reading.

2. *Predict how to answer the questions.* Students consider which of the four types of questions each question represents and the level of thinking required to answer each one.

3. *Read the text.* Students read the text while thinking about the questions they will answer afterwards.

4. *Answer the questions.* Students reread the questions, determine where to find the answers, locate the answers, and write them.

5. *Share answers.* Students read their answers aloud and explain how they answered the questions. Students should again refer to the type of question and whether the answer was "in the book" or "in the head."

APPLICATIONS AND EXAMPLES

An eighth-grade teacher asked his students to write examples of the four levels of questions in their reading logs as they read novels during literature circles and literature focus units. As students were reading *The Giver* (Lowry, 1993), the students wrote these questions and asked them during small-group and whole-class grand conversations:

Right There Questions
What was the first color Jonas could see?

How old did you have to be to get a bicycle?

What does a Receiver do?

Who was Rosemary?

Think and Search Questions
What does release mean?

How is Jonas different than the other people?

Why did Rosemary ask to be released?

Author and Me Questions
What was wrong with Jonas's Mom and Dad?

Was the Giver Jonas's real father?

What happened to Jonas and Gabe at the end of the book?

Was the Giver an honorable person?

On My Own Questions
Would you like to live in this community?
Could this happen in the United States?

Students can also write questions when reading informational books and content-area textbooks.

REFERENCES

Lowry, L. (1993). *The giver.* Boston: Houghton Mifflin.

Raphael, T., & McKinney, J. (1983). Examination of fifth- and eighth-grade children's question-answering behavior: An instructional study in metacognition. *Journal of Reading Behavior, 15,* 67–86.

Raphael, T., & Wonnacott, C. (1985). Heightening fourth grade students' sensitivity to sources of information for answering comprehension questions. *Reading Research Quarterly, 20,* 282–296.

Raphael, T. E. (1986). Teaching question-answer-relationships, revisited. *The Reading Teacher, 39,* 516–523.

32 Quickwrites and Quickdraws

- ● literature focus units
- ● literature circles
- ● reading-writing workshop
- ● thematic units

- ● preK
- ● K–2
- ● 3–5
- ● 6–8

- ● individual
- ○ pairs
- ○ small group
- ○ whole class

Students use quickwriting as they write in response to literature and for other types of impromptu writing. Students develop ideas, reflect on what they know about a topic, ramble on paper, and make connections among ideas (Tompkins, 2002). Quickdraws are a variation of quickwrites in which students draw instead of write. Young children often do quickdraws in which they draw pictures and add labels. Some students do a mixture of writing and drawing. Figure 32–1 presents a first grader's combination quickwrite and quickdraw made after reading *Sam, Bangs, and Moonshine* (Ness, 1966). In this Caldecott Medal story, a girl named Sam tells "moonshine" about a make-believe baby kangaroo to her friend Thomas. The results are almost disastrous. In the quickwrite, the child wrote, "If you lie, you will get in big trouble and you will hurt your friends."

Quickwriting was originally called freewriting and was popularized by Peter Elbow (1973) as a way to help students focus on exploring and developing ideas. Elbow's emphasis was on content rather than mechanics. Even by second or third grade, students have learned that many teachers emphasize correct spelling and careful handwriting more than the content of a composition. Elbow explains that focusing on mechanics makes writing "dead" because it does not allow students' natural voices to come through.

FIGURE 32–1 A First Grader's Quickwrite About *Sam, Bangs, and Moonshine*

STEP BY STEP

The steps in doing a quickwrite or a quickdraw are:

1. *Choose a topic.* Students identify a topic and write or draw on it for 5 to 10 minutes. They should focus on interesting ideas, make connections between the topic and their own lives, and reflect on their reading or learning.

2. *Share quickwrites.* Students share their quickwrites or quickdraws in small groups or during grand conversations, and then one student in each group shares with the class. Sharing also takes about 10 minutes, and the entire activity can be completed in approximately 20 minutes.

3. *Continue the process.* Students circle a key concept or important word in the quickwrite and then write another, more focused quickwrite. Or students can write more on their first quickwrite after listening to classmates share their quickwrites or after learning more about the topic.

APPLICATIONS AND EXAMPLES

Students do quickwrites and quickdraws for a variety of purposes in literature-based reading classrooms, including:

- as an entry for reading logs
- to define or explain a word on the word wall
- on the theme of story
- about a favorite character
- comparing book and film versions of a story
- about a favorite book during an author study
- about the characteristics of a literary genre
- about the project the student is creating

Students also do similar quickwrites and quickdraws during theme studies. Figure 32–2 shows a sixth grader's quickwrite during a unit on ancient Egypt. This quickwrite was written after a discussion comparing ancient and modern Egypt. As the class compared ancient and modern Egypt, the teacher made a Venn diagram on chart paper. Then students each made their own Venn diagram and referred to it as they wrote their quickwrites. In Figure 32–2, the student began by writing about the "reminders" of ancient Egypt that can be seen today; after listing some of the ways that the two Egypts are alike, she focused on a few of the differences. The purpose of this quickwrite was to reinforce what students are learning, not to write a comparison-contrast essay.

REFERENCES

Elbow, P. (1973). *Writing without teachers.* London: Oxford University Press.

Ness, E. (1966). *Sam, Bangs, and moonshine.* New York: Holt, Rinehart & Winston.

Tompkins, G. E. (2002). *Language arts: Content and teaching strategies* (5th ed.). Upper Saddle River, NJ: Merrill/Prentice Hall.

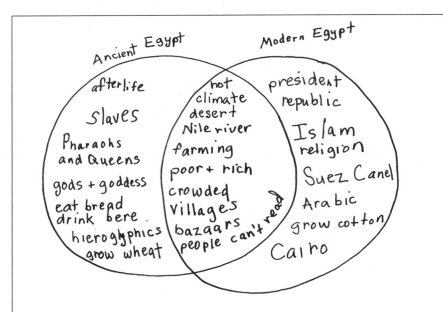

Ancient Egypt | Modern Egypt

afterlife
Slaves
Pharaohs
and Queens
gods + goddess
eat bread
drink bere
hieroglyphics
grow wheat

hot
climate
desert
Nile river
farming
poor + rich
crowded
villages
bazaars
people can't read

president
republic
Islam
religion
Suez Canel
Arabic
grow cotton
Cairo

Ancient Egypt began 5,000 years ago. That's a long time but you would see many reminds if you went there today. The pyramids are still in the dessert and the Nile river controls people's lives. The climate is the same to. Many people live in crouded villages and shop in bazaars. There are still many many poor people who cannot read and write. But there are big changes, too. Now there is a president instead of a pharoah and the people are Muslems. No one is a slave anymore but they are still poor.

FIGURE 32–2   A Sixth Grader's Quickwrite Comparing Ancient Egypt and Modern Egypt

Quilts

- ● literature focus units
- ● literature circles
- ● reading-writing workshop
- ● thematic units

- ● preK
- ● K–2
- ● 3–5
- ● 6–8

- ○ individual
- ○ pairs
- ● small group
- ● whole class

Students make construction paper squares and arrange them to make a quilt. These quilts are designed to highlight the theme and to celebrate a story that students have read during a literature focus unit (Tompkins, 2002). A square from a quilt about *Fly Away Home* (Bunting, 1991), a story about a homeless boy and his dad who live at the airport, is shown in Figure 33-1. The second graders created a modified "wedding ring" pattern for this quilt.

STEP BY STEP

The steps in making a quilt are:

1. *Design the quilt square.* Teachers and students choose a design for the quilt square that is appropriate for the story—its theme, characters, or setting. Students can choose a quilt design or create their own design that captures an important dimension of the story. They also choose symbolic colors for each shape in the quilt square.

2. *Make the squares.* Students each make a square and add a favorite sentence from the story or a comment about the story around the outside of the quilt square or in a designated section of the square.

3. *Assemble the quilt.* Teachers tape the squares together and back the quilt with butcher paper, or staple the squares side by side on a large bulletin board. The finished quilt for *Fly Away Home* is shown in Figure 33-2.

FIGURE 33–1 A Quilt Square About *Fly Away Home*

FIGURE 33–2   The Entire Quilt for *Fly Away Home*

APPLICATIONS AND EXAMPLES

Story quilts can be made of cloth, too. As an end-of-the-year project or to celebrate Book Week, teachers cut out squares of light-colored cloth and have students use fabric markers to draw pictures of their favorite stories and add the titles and authors. Then teachers or other adults sew the squares together, add a border, and complete the quilt. For more ideas about quiltmaking, check Mary Cobb's *The Quilt-Block History of Pioneer Days With Projects Kids Can Make* (1995).

REFERENCES

Bunting, E. (1991). *Fly away home.* New York: Clarion.

Cobb, M. (1995). *The quilt-block history of pioneer days with projects kids can make.* Brookfield, CT: Millbrook.

Tompkins, G. E. (2002). *Language arts: Content and teaching strategies* (5th ed.). Upper Saddle River, NJ: Merrill/Prentice Hall.

34 Read-Arounds

● literature focus units	○ preK	○ individual
● literature circles	● K–2	○ pairs
○ reading-writing workshop	● 3–5	● small group
● thematic units	● 6–8	● whole class

Students take turns reading favorite sentences and paragraphs from a story or other book during a read-around. Students often have read-arounds to celebrate the end of a literature focus unit and to bring closure to the book they have read and responded to. Students choose favorite passages from the book and reread them to prepare for the group activity. Then students take turns reading the passages aloud to classmates. The excerpts are not read in any particular order, and several students can read aloud the same passage if that is the one they have chosen to read. Read-arounds are social occasions, and students focus on memorable passages and particularly well-written sentences. Other names for read-arounds are popcorn reading and Quaker reading.

STEP BY STEP

The steps in doing a read-around are:

1. *Choose a favorite passage.* Students skim a book that they have already read to locate one or more favorite passages (a sentence or paragraph) and mark the passages with bookmarks or sticky notes.
2. *Practice reading the passage.* Students rehearse reading the passages once or twice so that they can read them fluently.
3. *Read the passages.* Teachers begin the read-around by asking a student to read a favorite passage aloud to the class. Then there is a pause and another student begins to read. Teachers don't call on students; any student may begin reading when no one else is reading. The passages can be read in any order, and more than one student can read the same passage. Teachers, too, read their favorite passages. Reading continues until everyone who wants to has read.

APPLICATIONS AND EXAMPLES

The passages students choose for read-arounds can be used for a variety of activities. Students can copy their favorite sentences on sentence strips or on posters to display in the classroom. Later, they can use the sentences as models for sentences they write. Or, they can use the sentences to examine sentence structure and identify the parts of a sentence.

Teachers can also use read-arounds with informational texts to review key concepts and important information. After reading a chapter from an informational book or a content-area textbook, teachers ask students to locate important and interesting information to read aloud. Then students take turns reading and rereading the sentences they selected. As students take turns reading the sentences aloud, they are reinforcing the important information presented in the book.

35 Readers Theatre

● literature focus units	○ preK	○ individual
○ literature circles	● K–2	○ pairs
○ reading-writing workshop	● 3–5	● small group
○ thematic units	● 6–8	○ whole class

Readers theatre is a dramatic production of a script by a group of readers. Students can read scripts in trade books and textbooks, or they can create their own scripts. They each assume a role and read the character's lines in the script. Readers interpret a story without using much action. They may stand or sit, but they must carry the whole communication of the plot, characterization, mood, and theme by using their voices, gestures, and facial expressions. Readers theatre avoids many of the restrictions inherent in theatrical productions: Students do not memorize their parts; elaborate props, costumes, and backdrops are not needed; and long, tedious hours are not spent rehearsing (Tompkins, 2002).

STEP BY STEP

The steps in readers theatre are:

1. *Select a script.* Students and the teacher select a script and then read and discuss it as they would any other story. Then students volunteer to read each part.

2. *Have students rehearse the production.* Students decide how to use their voice, gestures, and facial expressions to interpret the character they are reading. They read the script several times, striving for accurate pronunciation, voice projection, and appropriate inflections. Less rehearsal is needed for an informal, in-class presentation than for a more formal production; nevertheless, interpretations should always be developed as fully as possible.

3. *Stage the production.* Readers theatre can be presented on a stage or in a corner of the classroom. Students stand or sit in a row and read their lines in the script. They stay in position through the production or enter and leave according to the characters' appearances "onstage." If readers are sitting, they may stand to read their lines; if they are standing, they may step forward to read. The emphasis is not on production quality; rather, it is on the interpretive quality of the readers' voices and expressions. Costumes and props are unnecessary; however, adding a few small props can enhance interest and enjoyment as long as they do not interfere with the interpretive quality of the reading.

APPLICATIONS AND EXAMPLES

Teachers and students can create their own scripts for readers theatre. It is important to choose a story with a lot of conversation; any parts that don't include dialogue can become narrator parts. Depending on the number of narrator parts, one to four students can share the narrator duties. Teachers often make photocopies of the book for students to mark up or highlight as they develop the script. Sometimes students simply use their marked-up copies as the finished script, and at other times, teachers retype the finished script in script format and leave out unnecessary parts. The first page of a second-grade class's script for "The Elves and the Shoemaker" is shown in Figure 35–1.

FIGURE 35–1 The First Page of a Readers Theatre Script on "The Elves and the Shoemaker"

Characters

Narrator 1	Shoemaker	Lady 1	Elf 1
Narrator 2	Wife	Lady 2	Elf 2
Narrator 3	Man		Elf 3

Narrator 1: Once upon a time there was a good shoemaker and his wife, but they were very poor. The shoemaker had only one piece of leather to make into shoes.

Shoemaker: Tonight I will cut my last piece of leather to make a pair of shoes. I will make a pair of shiny black shoes for a man. Then I will sew the shoes in the morning.

Narrator 2: The next morning the shoemaker went to his work table but he couldn't believe what he saw.

Shoemaker: I can't believe my eyes. What a fine pair of shiny new shoes!

Wife: What did you say?

Shoemaker: Come and see what I see.

Wife: Who made these shiny new shoes?

Shoemaker: I do not know. It is like magic!

Narrator 3: At that very moment, a man came into the shoemaker's shop.

Man: Those shoes look just right for me. May I try them on?

Narrator 1: The man put on the shoes and they were just right for him.

Man: How much do these shiny new shoes cost?

Shoemaker: They cost one gold coin.

Man: Because I like them so much, I will give you two gold coins for the shoes.

Shoemaker: We are so fortunate! Now we can buy leather to make two more pairs of shoes.

REFERENCE

Tompkins, G. E. (2002). *Language arts: Content and teaching strategies* (5th ed.). Upper Saddle River, NJ: Merrill/Prentice Hall.

Reading Logs

36

- ● literature focus units
- ● literature circles
- ● reading-writing workshop
- ○ thematic units

- ○ preK
- ● K–2
- ● 3–5
- ● 6–8

- ● individual
- ○ pairs
- ○ small group
- ○ whole class

Reading logs are journals that students use to write their reactions and opinions about books they are reading or listening to the teacher read aloud. Through their reading log entries, students clarify misunderstandings, explore ideas, and deepen their comprehension of books they are reading (Barone, 1990; Hancock, 1992). They also add lists of words from the word wall, diagrams about story elements, and information about authors and genres (Tompkins, 2004). For a chapter book, students write after reading every chapter or two, and they often write single entries after reading picture books or short stories. Often students write a series of entries about a collection of books written by the same author, such as books by Eric Carle or Chris Van Allsburg, or about versions of the same folktale or fairy tale.

STEP BY STEP

The steps in using reading logs are:

1. *Prepare the reading logs.* Students make reading logs by stapling paper into booklets. After reading a story or other book or listening to it read aloud, students write the title of the book on a page in their reading logs. Sometimes they also write the name of the author. For a chapter book, students write the name of the chapter and the chapter number.

2. *Write entries.* Students write their reactions and reflections about the book or chapter. Instead of summarizing the book, students relate the books to their own lives or to other literature they have read. Students may also list interesting or unfamiliar words, jot down quotable quotes, and take notes about characters, plot, or other story elements. But the primary purpose of reading logs is for students to think about the book, connect literature to their lives, and develop their understanding of the story.

3. *Monitor students' entries.* Teachers check that students have completed assignments. They also write comments back to students about their interpretations and reflections. Because students' writing in reading logs is informal, teachers do not expect students to spell every word correctly, but it is not unreasonable to expect them to spell characters' names correctly and attempt to spell other words on the word wall correctly.

APPLICATIONS AND EXAMPLES

Students at all grade levels can write and draw reading log entries to help them comprehend the stories they are reading and listening to read aloud. Figure 36–1 presents a page from a third grader's reading log. In this entry, the student has responded to John Steptoe's *The Story of Jumping Mouse* (1984), a Native American legend about how a generous mouse was transformed into an eagle.

As a sixth-grade class read *The Giver* (Lowry, 1993), a Newbery Award–winning story of a not-so-perfect society, students discussed each chapter and brainstormed several possible titles for the chapter. Then they wrote entries in their reading logs and labeled each chapter with the number and the title they felt was most appropriate. The following three reading log entries show how a sixth grader grappled with the idea of "release." After reading and discussing Chapter 18, the student doesn't understand that "release" means "killing," but he grasps the awful meaning of the word as he reads Chapter 19.

The Story Of the Jumping Mouse
by John Steptoe

This story shows that it never hurts to help. And I think that the pictures are really good. My favorite part is when the mouse turned into an eagle. The mouse was the most generous.

FIGURE 36–1 A Third Grader's Reading Log Entry on *The Story of Jumping Mouse*

Chapter 18: "Release"

I think release is very rude. People have a right to live where they want to. Just because they're different they have to go somewhere else. I think release is when you have to go and live elsewhere. If you're released you can't come back to the community.

Chapter 19: "Release—The Truth"

It is so mean to kill people that didn't do anything bad. They kill perfectly innocent people. Everyone has a right to live. The shot is even worse to give them. They should be able to die on their own. If I were Jonas I would probably go insane. The people who kill the people that are to be released don't know what they're doing.

Chapter 20: "Mortified"

I don't think that Jonas is going to be able to go home and face his father. What can he do? Now that he knows what release is he will probably stay with The Giver for the rest of his life until he is released.

REFERENCES

Barone, D. (1990). The written responses of young children: Beyond comprehension to story understanding. *The New Advocate, 3,* 49–56.

Hancock, M. R. (1992). Literature response journals: Insights beyond the printed page. *Language Arts, 61,* 141–150.

Lowry, L. (1993). *The giver.* Boston: Houghton Mifflin.

Steptoe, J. (1984). *The story of Jumping Mouse.* New York: Morrow.

Tompkins, G. E. (2004). *Teaching writing: Balancing process and product* (4th ed.). Upper Saddle River, NJ: Merrill/Prentice Hall.

37 Reciprocal Questioning

○ literature focus units   ○ preK   ○ individual
○ literature circles   ○ K–2   ○ pairs
○ reading-writing workshop   ● 3–5   ● small group
● thematic units   ● 6–8   ● whole class

Teachers use reciprocal questioning to involve students more actively in reading and understanding informational texts. One type of reciprocal questioning, called ReQuest, was developed by Anthony Manzo (1969). In this instructional strategy, teachers segment content-area textbook chapters and informational books and articles into sentences or paragraphs, and teachers and students read a segment and ask each other questions about the text they have read. Students are encouraged to move beyond factual questions to think more deeply and critically about what they are reading. Types of questions that students and teachers ask during reciprocal questioning include:

- Questions about the meaning of particular words
- Questions that are answered directly in the text
- Questions that can be answered using common knowledge about the world
- Questions that relate the text to students' own lives
- "I wonder why" questions that go beyond the information provided in the text
- Questions that require students to locate information not contained in the text

Students read more purposefully when they read to create questions and to prepare to answer questions than when they read independently to finish an assignment.

STEP BY STEP

The steps in reciprocal questioning are:

1. *Prepare for the reciprocal questioning activity.* Students read the text and chunk it into segments. Teachers choose the length of a segment—from a sentence to a paragraph or two—depending on the complexity of the material being presented and students' reading levels.
2. *Introduce the assignment.* Teachers introduce the reading assignment and have students read silently a small segment of a content-area textbook chapter or informational book.
3. *Ask questions.* Students ask several questions about the text they have read; the teacher closes the book and answers the questions as fully as possible.
4. *Reverse roles.* This time, the teacher questions the students after they have closed their books. Teachers model asking a range of questions, from factual to interpretive questions. Or students and the teacher can alternate asking and answering questions after reading each segment of text.
5. *Repeat steps 2, 3, and 4 to read and discuss more of the text.* At an appropriate point, the teacher asks students to predict what information they expect to read and learn in the rest of the text, and then students continue reading the rest of the assignment independently.

APPLICATIONS AND EXAMPLES

Teachers use reciprocal questioning with books and other reading materials that students need extra support in order to read. For example, a teacher of fifth and sixth graders used reciprocal questioning

Page 1	What does "the real McCoy" mean?	S
	Have you ever said it?	S
	Who was Elijah McCoy?	S
	What did he invent?	S
Page 2	Was Elijah McCoy born in the United States?	T
	Do you think Elijah's parents ever knew Harriet Tubman?	T
	Was Elijah McCoy free or a slave?	T
Page 3	Did Elijah McCoy learn to read and write?	S
	What did Elijah McCoy like to do?	S
	Do you think he was a smart boy?	T
Page 4	Why did Elijah McCoy go to Scotland?	T
	What did he study in college?	T
Page 5	When did Elijah come to the United States?	S
	Why was it hard for him to get a job?	S
	What was the only job he could find?	S
Page 6	What does a fireman do on a train?	T
	Was it a good job?	S
Page 7	What was Elijah's other job?	S
	What does an oilman do?	S
Page 8	What was Elijah's invention?	T
	What does *lubrication* mean?	T
Page 9	What does *skeptical* mean?	S
	What does the saying "the real McCoy" mean?	T

FIGURE 37–1   Questions About *The Real McCoy: The Life of an African-American Inventor*

to read *The Real McCoy: The Life of an African-American Inventor* (Towle, 1993), an informational book about Elijah McCoy, whose name became an eponym. Because there is only a paragraph or two of text on each page of this picture book, it works well for reciprocal questioning. The teacher began by talking about words and phrases that came from people's names, such as *Levi's*. A list of the questions that students and the teacher asked is presented in Figure 37–1. Questions that students asked are marked with *S,* and questions asked by the teacher are marked with *T.* After the class read the first nine pages together, the teacher asked students to predict what the rest of the book was about and the students read the rest of the book independently. After reading, students made a lifeline of the events in this African-American inventor's life.

REFERENCES

Manzo, A. V. (1969). The ReQuest procedure. *Journal of Reading, 11,* 123–126.
Towle, W. (1993). *The real McCoy: The life of an African-American inventor.* New York: Scholastic.

Repeated Readings

● literature focus units	○ preK	● individual
○ literature circles	● K-2	○ pairs
● reading-writing workshop	● 3-5	○ small group
○ thematic units	○ 6-8	○ whole class

Teachers often encourage students to reread the featured book several times during literature focus units and to reread favorite books during reading workshop. Students become more fluent readers when they reread books, and each time they reread a book, their comprehension deepens (Yaden, 1988). Jay Samuels (1979) has also developed an instructional procedure to help students increase their reading fluency and accuracy through rereading.

STEP BY STEP

The steps in the repeated reading procedure are:

1. *Conduct a pretest.* Students choose a textbook or trade book and read a passage from the book aloud while the teacher records the reading times and any errors.
2. *Practice rereading the passage.* Students practice rereading the passage orally or silently several times.
3. *Conduct a posttest.* Students reread the passage while the teacher again records the reading times and notes any errors.
4. *Compare pre- and posttest results.* Students compare their reading times and accuracy between the first and last readings. Then the students prepare a graph to show their growth between first and last readings.

APPLICATIONS AND EXAMPLES

This procedure is useful for students who are slow and inaccurate readers. When teachers monitor students' readings on a regular basis, students will become more careful readers. Making a graph to document growth is an important component of the procedure.

REFERENCES

Samuels, J. (1979). The method of repeated readings. *The Reading Teacher, 32,* 403-408.
Yaden, D. B., Jr. (1988). Understanding stories through repeated read-alouds: How many does it take? *The Reading Teacher, 41,* 556-560.

39 Reports and Informational Books

- ● literature focus units
- ○ literature circles
- ● reading-writing workshop
- ● thematic units

- ○ preK
- ○ K–2
- ● 3–5
- ● 6–8

- ● individual
- ○ pairs
- ○ small group
- ○ whole class

Students write individual reports and informational books much like they write collaborative books: They design research questions, gather information to answer the questions, and compile what they have learned in a report. Writing individual reports demands two significant changes from class collaborations: First, students must narrow their topics; and second, they must assume the entire responsibility for writing the report (Tompkins, 2004).

STEP BY STEP

The steps in writing reports and informational books are:

1. *Choose and narrow topics.* Students choose topics for informational books and reports from a content-area unit, hobbies, or other interests. After choosing a general topic, such as cats or the solar system, they narrow the topic so that it is manageable. The broad topic of cats might be narrowed to pet cats or tigers, or the solar system might be narrowed to one planet.

2. *Design research questions.* Students design research questions by brainstorming a list of questions in their learning logs. They review the list, combine some questions, delete others, and finally arrive at four to six questions that are worthy of answering. When they begin their research, they may add new questions and delete others if they reach a dead end.

3. *Collect information.* Teachers assist students as they gather and organize information. Students use clusters (see p. 21) or data charts (see p. 27) to gather and organize information. Data charts, with their rectangular spaces for writing information, serve as a transition between clusters and notecards for upper-grade students.

4. *Draft the reports.* Students write a rough draft from the information they have gathered. Each research question can become a paragraph, a page, or a chapter in the report or informational book.

5. *Edit the reports.* Teachers work with students to revise and edit their books or reports. Students meet in writing groups to share their rough drafts and make revisions based on the feedback they receive from their classmates. After they revise, students use an editing checklist to proofread their reports and identify and correct mechanical errors.

6. *Publish the books or reports.* Students recopy their reports into books and add covers, a title page, a table of contents, and bibliographic information. Reports can also be published in several other ways—for example, as a filmstrip or video presentation, as a series of illustrated posters or dioramas, or as a dramatization.

APPLICATIONS AND EXAMPLES

Students often write informational books and reports as projects during literature focus units, writing workshop, and across-the-curriculum thematic units. Through these activities, students have opportunities to extend and personalize their learning and to practice using the writing process. As part of a science unit, seventh graders made picture books about the scientific concepts they were learning. One student made a book about "Solstices and Equinoxes," and one page from her book is shown in Figure 39–1.

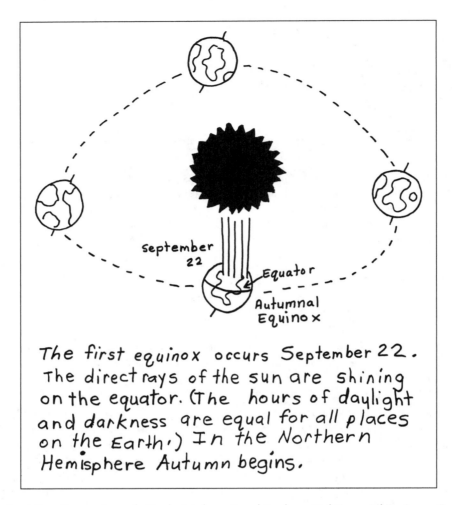

The first equinox occurs September 22.
The direct rays of the sun are shining
on the equator. (The hours of daylight
and darkness are equal for all places
on the Earth.) In the Northern
Hemisphere Autumn begins.

FIGURE 39–1   A Page From a Seventh Grader's Informational Book on "Solstices and Equinoxes"

REFERENCE

Tompkins, G. E. (2004). *Teaching writing: Balancing process and product* (4th ed.). Upper Saddle River, NJ:
    Merrill/Prentice Hall.

 **Shared Reading**

● literature focus units	● preK	○ individual
○ literature circles	● K–2	○ pairs
○ reading-writing workshop	● 3–5	● small group
● thematic units	● 6–8	● whole class

Teachers use shared reading to read books and other texts with students who could not read those books or texts independently (Holdaway, 1979). Students and the teacher read the text aloud and in unison. When doing shared reading with young children, teachers use enlarged texts, including big books, poems written on charts, language experience stories (see p. 53), and interactive writing charts (see p. 47), so that both small groups and whole-class groups can see the text and read along with the teacher. Teachers focus on concepts about print, including left-to-right direction of print, words, letters, and punctuation marks. Teachers model what fluent readers do as they involve students in enjoyable reading activities (Depree & Iversen, 1996; Fountas & Pinnell, 1996).

Shared reading is a step between reading to children and independent reading by students (Parkes, 2000; Slaughter, 1993). For older students, teachers use shared reading techniques to read books that students could not read themselves. Students each have a copy of the text—a chapter book, content-area textbook, or other book—and the teacher and students read together. The teacher or another fluent reader reads aloud while other students follow along in the text, reading to themselves.

STEP BY STEP

The steps in shared reading are:

1. *Introduce the text.* Teachers talk about the book or other text by activating or building background knowledge on topics related to the book and by reading the title and the author's name aloud.

2. *Read the text aloud.* Teachers read the story aloud to students, using a pointer (a dowel rod with a pencil eraser on the end) to track as they read. They invite students to join in the reading if the story is repetitive.

3. *Have a grand conversation* (see p. 39). Teachers invite students to talk about the story, ask questions, and share their responses.

4. *Reread the story.* Students take turns turning pages and using the pointer to track the reading. Teachers invite students to join in reading familiar and predictable words. Also, they take opportunities to teach and use graphophonic cues and reading strategies while reading.

 ELL The shared reading experience is useful for students learning English because they have multiple opportunities to listen to the teacher or another fluent English speaker reading aloud while they follow along, looking at the words. In addition, they are encouraged to join in and read familiar words when they can, but there is no pressure to perform.

5. *Continue the process.* Teachers continue to reread the story with students several more times over a period of several days, again having students turn pages and take turns using the pointer to track the text while reading. They encourage students who can read the text to read along with them.

6. *Have students read independently.* After students become familiar with the text, teachers distribute individual copies of the book or other text for students to read independently and use for a variety of activities.

APPLICATIONS AND EXAMPLES

Teachers use the reading process for shared reading lessons. The reading process involves five stages: prereading, reading, responding, exploring, and applying (Tompkins, 2003). During the prereading stage, teachers introduce the book and interest students in reading. Next, teachers use shared reading for the first reading of the book, and students respond to the book through grand conversations and writing in reading logs. Then students reread the story with buddies and independently during the exploring stage and create projects during the applying stage. Figure 40–1 shows a plan for shared reading using *Hattie and the Fox* by Mem Fox (1986).

In addition to using shared reading to read big books, teachers use shared reading in choral reading (see p. 15) and readers theatre (see p. 84). They also use shared reading when they read a chapter book together if all students are reading along in their copies of the book as the teacher or another student reads aloud.

FIGURE 40–1 A Plan for Shared Reading Using *Hattie and the Fox*

Stage	Activities
Prereading	Teachers review several books students have already read in which foxes are main characters, including *Rosie's Walk* (Hutchins, 1968) and *The Gingerbread Boy* (Galdone, 1975), and they explain that students will read another book about a fox today. They set a big book version of the story on the easel, show the cover of the book, and read the title: *Hattie and the Fox* (Fox, 1986). Teachers ask students to predict what will happen in this book.
Reading	Teachers use shared reading to read aloud the big book version of the story. They use a pointer so that students can track the text, and they encourage students to join in repeating the refrain and other familiar and predictable words. After reading the story once, students often want to read the story a second time, and they join in more of the reading. Students also take turns using the pointer.
Responding	Students and the teacher talk about the story and the surprise ending in a grand conversation. After the discussion, students write responses in reading logs.
Exploring	Students participate in a variety of exploring activities. They add words to the word wall, participate at literacy center activities, and reread the big book version for several days. Then they read small versions of the book with partners and independently.
Applying	Students create projects to extend their understanding of the story. They might make puppets to use in story retellings, write letters to Mem Fox, the author of the story, or write their own fox stories.

REFERENCES

Depree, H., & Iversen, S. (1996). *Early literacy in the classroom: A new standard for young readers.* Bothell, WA: Wright Group.

Fountas, I. C., & Pinnell, G. S. (1996). *Guided reading: Good first teaching for all children.* Portsmouth, NH: Heinemann.

Fox, M. (1986). *Hattie and the fox.* New York: Bradbury Press.

Galdone, P. (1975). *The gingerbread boy.* New York: Seabury.

Holdaway, D. (1979). *Foundations of literacy.* Auckland, NZ: Ashton Scholastic.

Hutchins, P. (1968). *Rosie's walk.* New York: Macmillan.

Parkes, B. (2000). *Read it again! Revisiting shared reading.* York, ME: Stenhouse.

Slaughter, J. (1993). *Beyond storybooks: Young children and the shared book experience.* Newark, DE: International Reading Association.

Tompkins, G. E. (2003). *Literacy for the 21st century* (3rd ed.). Upper Saddle River, NJ: Merrill/Prentice Hall.

Sketch-to-Stretch

- ● literature focus units
- ● literature circles
- ○ reading-writing workshop
- ○ thematic units

- ○ preK
- ● K–2
- ● 3–5
- ● 6–8

- ● individual
- ○ pairs
- ○ small group
- ○ whole class

Sketch-to-stretch is a visually representing activity that moves students beyond literal comprehension to think more deeply about the characters, theme, and other elements of story structure and the author's craft in a story they are reading (Harste, Short, & Burke, 1988). Students work in small groups to draw pictures or diagrams to represent what the story means to them, not pictures of their favorite character or episode. In their sketches, students use lines, shapes, colors, symbols, and words to express their interpretations and feelings. Because students work in a social setting with the support of classmates, they share ideas with each other, extend their understanding, and generate new insights (Whitin, 1994, 1996).

STEP BY STEP

The steps in sketch-to-stretch are:

1. *Read and respond to a story.* Students read a story or several chapters of a longer book, and they respond to the story in a grand conversation (see p. 39) or in reading logs (see p. 86).

2. *Discuss the themes.* Students and the teacher talk about the themes in the story and ways to symbolize meanings. Teachers remind students that there are many ways to represent the meaning of an experience, and that students can use lines, colors, shapes, symbols, and words to visually represent what a story means to them. Students and the teacher talk about possible meanings and ways they might visually represent these meanings.

3. *Draw the sketches.* Students work in small groups to draw sketches that reflect what the story means to them. Teachers emphasize that students should focus on the meaning of the story, not their favorite part, and that there is no single correct interpretation of the story.

4. *Share the sketches.* Students meet in small groups to share their sketches and talk about the symbols they used. Teachers encourage classmates to study each student's sketch and tell what they think the student is trying to convey.

5. *Share some sketches with the class.* Each group chooses one sketch from their group to share with the class.

6. *Revise sketches and make final copies.* Some students will want to revise and add to their sketches based on feedback they received and ideas from classmates. Also, students make final copies if the sketches are being used as projects.

APPLICATIONS AND EXAMPLES

Students need many opportunities to experiment with this activity before they move beyond drawing pictures of the story events or characters and are able to think symbolically. It is helpful to introduce this teaching strategy through a minilesson (see p. 67) and to draw several sketches together as a class before students do their own sketches. By drawing several sketches, students learn that there is no single correct interpretation, and teachers help students focus on the interpretation rather than on their artistic talents (Ernst, 1993). Figure 41–1 shows a fourth grader's sketch-to-stretch made after reading *The Ballad of Lucy Whipple* (Cushman, 1996), a story set during the California gold rush. The sketch-to-stretch emphasizes one of the themes of the book—that you make your own happiness, or that home is where you are.

FIGURE 41–1 A Fourth Grader's Sketch-to-Stretch on *The Ballad of Lucy Whipple*

REFERENCES

Cushman, K. (1996). *The ballad of Lucy Whipple.* New York: Clarion.

Ernst, K. (1993). *Picturing learning.* Portsmouth, NH: Heinemann.

Harste, J. C., Short, K. G., & Burke, C. (1988). *Creating classrooms for authors: The reading-writing connection.* Portsmouth, NH: Heinemann.

Whitin, P. E. (1994). Opening potential: Visual response to literature. *Language Arts, 71,* 101–107.

Whitin, P. E. (1996). *Sketching stories, stretching minds.* Portsmouth, NH: Heinemann.

SQ3R Study Strategy

○ literature focus units	○ preK	● individual
○ literature circles	○ K–2	○ pairs
○ reading-writing workshop	○ 3–5	○ small group
● thematic units	● 6–8	○ whole class

In the SQ3R study strategy (Anderson & Armbruster, 1984), students use five steps—survey, question, read, recite, and review—to read and remember information in content-area reading assignments. Because this strategy is very effective when students apply it correctly, it is important that teachers teach students how to apply the steps and provide opportunities for students to practice using the strategy correctly.

STEP BY STEP

The five steps in the SQ3R study strategy are:

1. *Survey.* Students survey or preview the reading assignment, noting headings and skimming, or rapidly reading, the introduction and summary. They note the main ideas that are presented. This step helps students activate prior knowledge and organize what they will read.
2. *Question.* Students turn each heading into a question before reading the section. Reading to find the answer to the question gives students a purpose for reading.
3. *Read.* Students read the section to find the answers to the questions they have formulated. They read each section separately.
4. *Recite.* Immediately after reading each section, students recite from memory the answer to the question they formulated and other important information they have read. Students can answer the questions orally or in writing.
5. *Review.* After they finish the entire reading assignment, students take a few minutes to review what they have read. They ask themselves the questions they developed from each heading and try to recall the answers they learned by reading. If students took notes or wrote answers to the questions in step 4, they should try to review without referring to the written notes. If students answered the questions orally in step 4, they can write the answers now.

APPLICATIONS AND EXAMPLES

Students use the SQ3R study strategy when they are reading content-area textbooks and want to remember what they are reading. Seventh and eighth graders and their teacher developed the chart shown in Figure 42–1 as they learned to use the SQ3R study strategy.

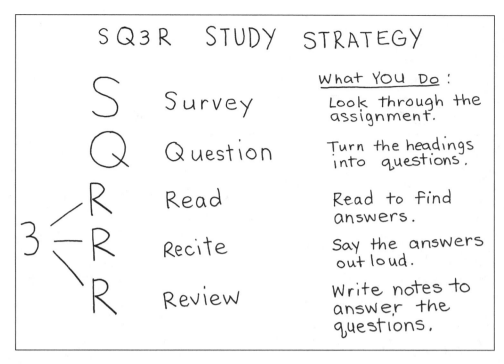

FIGURE 42–1   An Upper-Grade Class Chart on the SQ3R Study Strategy

REFERENCE

Anderson, T. H., & Armbruster, B. B. (1984). Studying. In P. D. Pearson, R. Barr, M. L. Kamil, & P. Mosenthal (Eds.), *Handbook of reading research* (pp. 657–679). New York: Longman.

Story Boards

- ● literature focus units
- ○ literature circles
- ○ reading-writing workshop
- ● thematic units

- ● preK
- ● K–2
- ● 3–5
- ● 6–8

- ● individual
- ● pairs
- ● small group
- ● whole class

Story boards are cards on which the illustrations and text from a picture book have been attached (Tompkins, 2003). Teachers make story boards by cutting apart two copies of a picture book and gluing the pages on pieces of tagboard. The most important use of story boards is to sequence the events of a story by lining the story boards on a chalkboard tray or hanging the cards on a clothesline. Once the pages of the picture book have been laid out, students visualize the story and its structure in new ways and closely examine the illustrations. For example, students arrange story boards from *Barn Dance!* (Martin & Archambault, 1986) or *If You Give a Mouse a Cookie* (Numeroff, 1985) in a circle to emphasize the structure of the story. Or, they identify the beginning, middle, and end and recognize the passing of the seasons in *Sylvester and the Magic Pebble* (Steig, 1969). Students notice that the weather outside the window changes as *The Napping House* (Wood, 1984) progresses, and they pick out the dream sequences in the middle of *Hey, Al* (Yorinks, 1986) and *Abuela* (Dorros, 1991). Students also use story boards to compare versions of folktales and other stories, such as *The Mitten* (Brett, 1989; Tresselt, 1964), *The Old Man's Mitten* (Pollock, 1986), and *The Woodcutter's Mitten* (Koopmans, 1990).

STEP BY STEP

The steps in making story boards are:

1. *Collect two copies of a book.* It is preferable to use paperback copies of the books because they are less expensive to purchase. In a few picture books, all the illustrations are on right-hand or left-hand pages, so only one copy is needed. For example, in Chris Van Allsburg's *The Mysteries of Harris Burdick* (1984), all illustrations are on the right-hand pages.

2. *Cut the books apart.* Teachers remove the covers and separate the pages. Next, they even out the edges of the cut-apart sides.

3. *Attach the pages to pieces of cardboard.* Teachers glue each page or double-page spread to a piece of cardboard, making sure that pages from each book are alternated so that each page in the story will be included.

4. *Laminate the cards.* Teachers laminate the cards so that they can withstand use by students.

5. *Use the cards in sequencing activities.* Teachers use the story board cards for a variety of activities, including sequencing and word-study activities.

 Story boards are useful tools for English learners. They use story boards to preview a story before reading to get the gist of the story, they sequence a set of story boards after reading to review the events in a story, and they draw story boards after reading because they can often share their understanding better through art than through language.

APPLICATIONS AND EXAMPLES

Students can use story boards for a variety of activities. For example, they use the cards in sequencing activities. Teachers pass out the cards in a random order to students, and students line up around the classroom to sequence the story events. Teachers can also pass out story boards for read-arounds and tea party activities.

 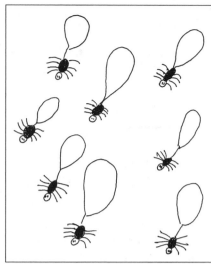

FIGURE 43–1   Story Boards Illustrating Two Chapters in *Charlotte's Web*

Story boards can also be used when there are only a few copies of a picture book so that students can identify words for the word wall, notice literary language, and examine the illustrations. Students can write words and sentences on sticky notes and attach them to story boards.

For chapter books, students can create their own story boards, one for each chapter. Students divide into small groups, and each group works on a different chapter. Students make a poster with a picture illustrating the chapter, and they can also write a paragraph-length summary of the chapter. Two story boards made by third graders while listening to their teacher read *Charlotte's Web* aloud are shown in Figure 43–1.

REFERENCES

Brett, J. (1989). *The mitten.* New York: Putnam.

Dorros, A. (1991). *Abuela.* New York: Dutton.

Koopmans, L. (1990). *The woodcutter's mitten.* New York: Crocodile Books.

Martin, B., Jr., & Archambault, J. (1986). *Barn dance!* New York: Henry Holt.

Numeroff, L. (1985). *If you give a mouse a cookie.* New York: Harper & Row.

Pollock, Y. (1986). *The old man's mitten.* Greenvale, NY: Mondo Publishing.

Steig, W. (1969). *Sylvester and the magic pebble.* New York: Simon & Schuster.

Tompkins, G. E. (2003). *Literacy for the 21st century* (3rd ed.). Upper Saddle River, NJ: Prentice Hall.

Tresselt, A. (1964). *The mitten.* New York: Scholastic.

Van Allsburg, C. (1984). *The mysteries of Harris Burdick.* Boston: Houghton Mifflin.

White, E. B. (1952). *Charlotte's web.* New York: HarperCollins.

Wood, A. (1984). *The napping house.* New York: Harcourt Brace Jovanovich.

Yorinks, A. (1986). *Hey, Al.* New York: Farrar, Straus & Giroux.

Story Retelling

● literature focus units	● preK	● individual
○ literature circles	● K–2	● pairs
○ reading-writing workshop	● 3–5	● small group
○ thematic units	○ 6–8	○ whole class

Teachers use story retelling to assess students' comprehension of a story (Gambrell, Pfeiffer, & Wilson, 1985; Morrow, 1985). Students retell the story orally or in writing, and oral story retelling is especially useful with emergent readers. Teachers ask students to retell the story in their own words. Sometimes the teacher invites students to use puppets, small objects, or flannel board pieces, turns the pages through a picture book, or uses story boards to prompt them. Students retell everything they remember about a story; afterwards the teacher asks questions to prompt their memory, such as "What else can you remember?" and "What happened next?" As students retell the story, the teacher takes notes to analyze how many ideas the class has remembered.

When students retell stories in writing, they make small books and write the beginning on one page, the middle on one or more pages, and the end on another page. They write the story in their own words and draw pictures to accompany their words. Figure 44–1 shows a first grader's beginning page of a retelling of *Katy No-Pocket* (Payne, 1969), the story of kangaroo who doesn't have a pocket and has to find another way to carry her joey. As students retell stories orally or in writing, they organize story information and events, develop fluency in composing stories, and reinforce their concept of story.

 STEP BY STEP

The steps in story retelling are:

1. *Prepare a story retelling guide.* Teachers prepare a story retelling guide to use in recording and analyzing the ideas that students recall. Figure 44-2 presents a sample story retelling guide.

2. *Read the story.* Teachers read a story with students and provide a variety of activities in which students discuss and explore the story.

3. *Retell the story.* Teachers ask students to retell the story orally or in writing. They provide manipulative materials such as puppets, objects related to the book, story boards, or a copy of the book for students to use as they retell the story. Story retelling activities can be done individually or in small groups.

4. *Help students retell the story.* If students have difficulty retelling the story, teachers prompt them by asking one or more of these questions:

   How did the story begin?

   Who was the story about?

   What happened at the beginning?

   When did the story happen?

   Where did the story happen?

   What happened next?

   What did _____ do next?

   How did the story end? (Morrow, 1985)

   These prompts can be used when students retell stories orally or in writing.

5. *Mark the retelling guide.* Teachers mark the story retelling guide as students retell stories orally or when reading students' written retellings. They make notes about the students' unaided

FIGURE 44–1 The First Page of a First Grader's Written Retelling of *Katy No-Pocket*

Katy No - Pocket

Katy could not carry him. She had no Pocket. She cride and cride.

retelling in the column on the left side and add the student's prompted responses in the right column. Then they analyze students' retelling and determine how many ideas the students recalled in the beginning, middle, and end of the story. In this way, teachers track students' retellings and document their progress.

APPLICATIONS AND EXAMPLES

Teachers can customize the story retelling guide by making a list of the main ideas and details of a story. It is useful to divide the story into segments to organize the retelling, and the three parts—beginning, middle, and end—work well for most stories. A first-grade teacher identified these ideas for *Hey, Al* (Yorinks, 1986):

Beginning: *Al was a janitor.*
              His dog was named Eddie.
              They lived in a small city apartment.
              They worked hard.
              A bird offered Al an easy life.

Middle: *Al and Eddie went with the bird.*
              The bird flew them to a paradise island.
              They ate and swam.
              They had it good.
              They started to turn into birds.
              They wanted to go home.

Name _____ Date _____

Story _____

Student's familiarity with the story:

one reading •————•————•————•————• many readings

Part	Student's Unaided Retelling	Prompts	Student's Aided Retelling
Beginning		What happened at the beginning? Where did the story take place? Who were the characters? What was the main problem?	
Middle		What happened in the middle? What happened next? What did _____ do?	
End		How was the problem solved? What happened at the end? What was the author's message?	

FIGURE 44–2 Story Retelling Sheet

Unaided Retelling	Story Retelling Guide for *Hey, Al* Student _____ Date _____	Prompted Retelling
	Al was a janitor. His dog was named Eddie. They lived in a small city apartment. They worked hard. A bird offered Al an easy life.	
	Al and Eddie went with the bird. The bird flew them to a paradise island. They ate and swam. They had it good. They started to turn into birds. They wanted to go home.	
	They started to fly back home. Al made it back to the city. Eddie fell into the sea. Al was heartbroken. Eddie was able to swim back home. Al was so happy to see Eddie. They learned to make their own happiness.	

FIGURE 44–3   A First-Grade Story Retelling Guide for *Hey, Al*

End:
> They started to fly back home.
> Al made it back to the city.
> Eddie fell into the sea.
> Al was heartbroken.
> Eddie was able to swim back home.
> Al was so happy to see Eddie.
> They learned to make their own happiness.

Then the teacher made a story retelling guide and listed these ideas, as shown in Figure 44–3. The teacher checked off the ideas that students recalled without prompting in the left column; in the right column, the teacher noted which ideas students recalled with prompting. Later the teacher analyzed students' retelling of the story.

REFERENCES

Gambrell, L. B., Pfeiffer, W., & Wilson, R. (1985). The effect of retelling upon reading comprehension and recall of text information. *Journal of Educational Research, 78,* 216–220.

Morrow, L. M. (1985). Retelling stories: A strategy for improving children's comprehension, concept of story structure, and oral language complexity. *Elementary School Journal, 85,* 647–661.

Payne, E. (1969). *Katy No-Pocket.* Boston: Houghton Mifflin.

Yorinks, A. (1986). *Hey, Al.* New York: Farrar, Straus & Giroux.

Sustained Silent Reading (SSR)

○ literature focus unit	○ preK	○ individual
○ literature circles	● K–2	○ pairs
● reading-writing workshop	● 3–5	○ small groups
○ thematic units	● 6–8	● whole class

Sustained silent reading (SSR) is an independent reading time set aside during the school day for students in one class or the entire school to silently read self-selected books. In some schools, everyone—students, teachers, principals, secretaries, and custodians—stops to read, usually for a 15- to 30-minute period. SSR is a popular reading activity in schools that is known by a variety of names, including "drop everything and read" (DEAR), "sustained quiet reading time" (SQUIRT), and "our time to enjoy reading" (OTTER).

Teachers use SSR to increase the amount of reading students do every day and to develop their ability to read silently and without interruption (Hunt, 1967; McCracken & McCracken, 1978). Through numerous studies, SSR has been found to be beneficial in developing students' reading ability (Krashen, 1993; Pilgreen, 2000). In addition, it promotes a positive attitude toward reading and encourages students to develop the habit of daily reading. Because students choose the books they will read, they have the opportunity to develop their own tastes and preferences as readers. SSR is based on these guidelines:

1. Students choose the books they read.
2. Students read silently.
3. The teacher serves as a model by reading during SSR.
4. Students choose one book or other reading material for the entire reading time.
5. The teacher sets a timer for a predetermined, uninterrupted time period, usually ranging between 15 and 30 minutes.
6. All students in the class or school participate.
7. Students do not write book reports or participate in other after-reading activities.
8. The teacher does not keep records or evaluate students on their performance. (Pilgreen, 2000)

To have a successful SSR program, students need to have access to lots of books in a classroom library or the school library and know how to use the Goldilocks strategy (see p. 37) to choose books at their reading level. If students don't have books that interest them written at their reading level, they won't be able to read independently for extended periods of time.

STEP BY STEP

The steps in sustained silent reading are:

1. *Set aside a time for SSR.* Teachers allow time every day for uninterrupted, independent reading. It may last for only 10 minutes in a first-grade classroom or 20 to 30 minutes or more in the upper grades. Teachers often begin with a 10-minute period and then extend the SSR period as students build endurance and ask for more time.

2. *Ensure that students have books to read.* For capable readers, SSR is a time for independent reading. Students keep a book at their desks to read during SSR and use a bookmark to mark their place in the book. Beginning readers may read new books or choose three or four leveled readers that they have already read to reread during SSR. For children who cannot read on their own, partner reading may be substituted for independent reading.

3. *Set a timer for a predetermined time.* Teachers keep a kitchen timer in the classroom, and after everyone gets out a book to read, set the timer for the SSR reading period. To ensure that students are not disturbed during SSR, some teachers place a "do not disturb" sign on the door.

4. *Read along with students.* Teachers read a book, magazine, or newspaper for pleasure while students read. This way teachers model what capable readers do and that reading is a pleasurable activity.

Even though SSR was specifically developed without follow-up activities, many teachers use a few carefully selected and brief follow-up activities to sustain students' interest in reading books (Pilgreen, 2000). Students often discuss their reading with a partner, or volunteers give book talks to tell the whole class about their books. As students listen to one another, they get ideas about books that they might like to read in the future. Sometimes students develop a ritual of passing on the books they have finished reading to interested classmates.

APPLICATIONS AND EXAMPLES

When all teachers in a school are working together to set up an SSR time, they meet to set a daily time for this special reading activity and lay the ground rules for the program. Many schools have SSR first thing in the morning or at some other convenient time during the day. What is most important is that SSR is held every day at the same time, and that everyone in the school—children and adults—stop what they are doing to read. If teachers use the time to grade papers or work with individual students, the program won't be effective. The principal and other staff members should also make a habit of visiting a different classroom each day to join in the reading activity.

REFERENCES

Hunt, L. (1967). Evaluation through teacher-pupil conferences. In T. C. Barrett (Ed.), *The evaluation of children's reading achievement* (pp. 111–126). Newark, DE: International Reading Association.

Krashen, S. (1993). *The power of reading.* Englewood, CO: Libraries Unlimited.

McCracken, R., & McCracken, M. (1978). Modeling is the key to sustained silent reading. *The Reading Teacher, 31,* 406–408.

Pilgreen, J. L. (2000). *The SSR handbook: How to organize and manage a sustained silent reading program.* Portsmouth, NH: Boynton/Cook/Heinemann.

46

Tea Party

● literature focus units	○ preK	○ individual
○ literature circles	● K–2	○ pairs
○ reading-writing workshop	● 3–5	○ small group
● thematic units	● 6–8	● whole class

Students and the teacher participate in a tea party to read or reread excerpts from a story, informational book, or content-area textbook. Sometimes teachers have students reread favorite excerpts to celebrate a book they have finished reading, or they use tea party to introduce a new chapter in a content-area textbook. Teachers make several copies of selected excerpts, back them with tagboard, and laminate them. Then students move around the classroom, reading their cards to each other and talking about the excerpt they have read.

Tea party is similar to read-arounds (see p. 83) in that students read excerpts from books and other reading materials. However, these two literacy strategies often serve different instructional purposes: Teachers usually select the excerpts that students read for tea party to introduce or review important concepts, summarize the events in a story, or focus on an element of story structure, whereas students choose the excerpts that are particularly meaningful to them for read-arounds. Also, students are more active, moving around the classroom and socializing with individual classmates during tea party, whereas students remain seated and share with the whole class during read-arounds.

STEP BY STEP

The steps in tea party are:

1. *Make the cards.* Teachers make cards with excerpts from a story, informational book, or content-area textbook that students are reading. They laminate the cards, or use sentence strips or story boards with younger students.

2. *Practice reading.* Students practice reading the excerpts to themselves several times until they can read them fluently.

3. *Share excerpts.* Students move around the classroom, stopping to read their excerpts to other students. When students pair up, they take turns reading their excerpts. After the first student reads, both students discuss the text; then the other student reads and both students comment on the second student's text. Then students move apart and find other classmates to read their cards to.

4. *Share excerpts with the class.* Students return to their desks after 10 to 15 minutes, and teachers invite several students to read their excerpts to the class or talk about what they learned through the tea party activity.

APPLICATIONS AND EXAMPLES

Tea party is a good way to celebrate the conclusion of a literature focus unit or a thematic unit. Students can pick the excerpts they want to read, and the tea party activity reinforces the main ideas taught during the unit. Teachers also use tea party to introduce a thematic unit by taking excerpts from informational books or content-area textbooks that present the main ideas and key vocabulary to be taught during the unit. Figure 46–1 shows six tea party cards from a class set that a seventh-grade teacher used to introduce a unit on ecology. The teacher collected some of the sentences and paragraphs from informational books and a textbook chapter that students would read, and she wrote other selections herself. One or two key words are highlighted on each card to help students focus their attention on key words. Students read and discussed the excerpts and began a word wall with the key words. These two activities activated students' background knowledge about ecology and began to build new concepts.

FIGURE 46–1 Tea Party Cards With Information About Ecology

Recycling means using materials over and over or making them into new things instead of throwing them away.

Acid rain happens when poisonous gases from factories and cars get into rain clouds. Then the gases mix with rain and fall back to earth. It is harmful to our environment and to the people and animals on earth.

Plastic bottles, plastic forks, and plastic bags last forever! A big problem with plastic is that it doesn't **biodegrade.** Instead of filling landfills with plastic, it should be recycled.

Many cities have air filled with pollution called **smog.** This pollution is so bad that the sky looks brown, not blue.

The **ozone layer** around the earth protects us from the harmful rays of the sun. This layer is being damaged by gases called chlorofluorocarbons or **CFCs.** These gases are used in air conditioners, fire extinguishers, and styrofoam.

Americans cut down 850 million trees last year to make **paper products.** Sound like a lot of trees? Consider this: One tree can be made into approximately 700 grocery bags, and a large grocery store uses about that many bags in an hour!

47 Venn Diagrams

● literature focus units	○ preK	● individual
○ literature circles	● K–2	● pairs
○ reading-writing workshop	● 3–5	● small group
● thematic units	● 6–8	● whole class

Venn diagrams have two (or more) overlapping circles, and students use these charts to compare and contrast topics. Students write and draw the differences in the parts of the circles that do not overlap and the similarities in the overlapping section. Sometimes teachers draw large Venn diagrams on chart paper and have the class work together to add the similarities and differences; otherwise, students work individually or in small groups to make Venn diagrams on construction paper. To save the time involved in carefully drawing and overlapping the circles to make a Venn diagram, teachers often use pizza pans as patterns to draw Venn diagrams on sheets of poster board and then laminate the sheets. Students use water-based pens designed for overhead projector transparencies to write on the laminated Venn diagrams, and they can be used over and over.

Venn diagrams are useful because they help students think more deeply and analytically about what they are reading and learning. For example, during a literature focus unit, students can compare and contrast two characters or compare the book and video versions of a book using a Venn diagram. Figure 47–1 shows a Venn diagram created by a second grader to compare two versions of *The Town Mouse and the Country Mouse,* one written by Lorinda Cauley (1984) and the other by Jan Brett (1994). Making a Venn diagram may complete the activity, or it may serve as prewriting for a writing activity.

STEP BY STEP

The steps in making a Venn diagram are:

1. *Compare and contrast the topics.* Teachers discuss the similarities and differences between two topics with students. Some topics have more similarities, and others have more differences. Teachers think about the comparisons and contrasts ahead of time so that they can support students in their thinking. Teachers often ask questions to help students make the comparisons and contrasts. For example, when discussing *The Town Mouse and the Country Mouse,* the teacher of first and second graders asked these questions:

   Did the two mice look the same?

   Did the Town Mouse and the Country Mouse eat the same food or different food?

   What did the Country Mouse want?

   What did the Town Mouse want?

2. *Draw a Venn diagram.* Teachers draw a Venn diagram on a sheet of butcher paper, a sheet of poster board, or on sheets of construction paper and label the two circles with the names of the topics. Sometimes teachers add pictures along with the labels.

3. *Fill in the diagram.* In the outer parts of the two circles, students write words and phrases and draw pictures representing the differences between the two topics. Then they write and draw about the similarities in the overlapping part of the circles.

4. *Summarize the information.* Teachers summarize the information presented on the Venn diagram, and support students in interpreting the information. The first and second graders who made the Venn diagram on the two versions of *The Town Mouse and the Country Mouse* concluded that the two books were more alike than they were different.

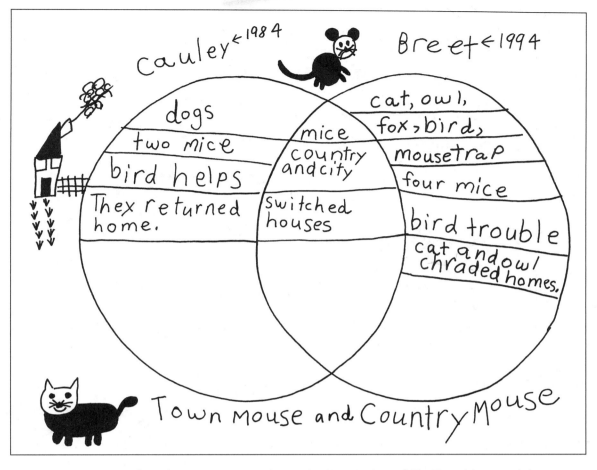

FIGURE 47–1 A Second Grader's Venn Diagram Comparing Two Versions of *The Town Mouse and the Country Mouse*

5. *Display the Venn diagram.* Teachers post the completed Venn diagram in the classroom and use the information on the chart for other activities. For example, students can use information from the Venn diagram in writing a comparison-contrast essay or an opinion essay.

APPLICATIONS AND EXAMPLES

Venn diagrams can be used in a variety of ways in literature focus units and in thematic units. Some ways to use Venn diagrams in literature focus units are to compare and contrast:

two characters
the book and the video version of the book
a book and its sequel
two books with similar themes
two books by the same author
two authors or illustrators

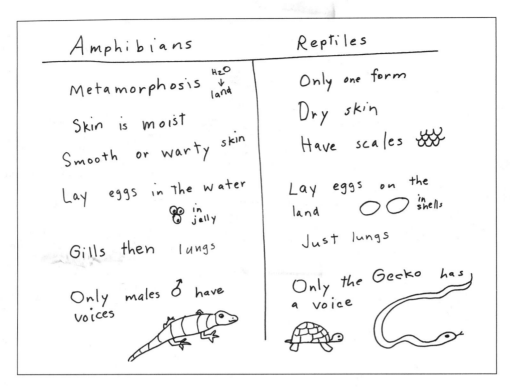

FIGURE 47–2 A Sixth Grader's T-Chart Contrasting Reptiles and Amphibians

In thematic units, Venn diagrams are used to compare and contrast:

> life in the Middle Ages and life today
> the earth and another planet in the solar system
> the Oregon Trail and the Santa Fe Trail
> baleen and toothed whales
> deciduous and evergreen trees
> ancient Egyptian and ancient Greek civilizations
> the American Revolution and the Civil War
> Thanksgiving in colonial times and today

Even kindergarten students can use Venn diagrams. During a unit on pets in one kindergarten class, students signed their names on a Venn diagram to describe themselves as "dog lovers" or "cat lovers." Students who said they loved both kinds of pets signed their names in the overlapping circles.

Venn diagrams are used to both compare and contrast two topics; when teachers want only to contrast two topics, such as reptiles and amphibians, plant-eating and meat-eating dinosaurs, or the Arctic and the Antarctic, T-charts are more effective than Venn diagrams. To make a T-chart, draw a large capital letter T and write the two topics above the horizontal stroke of the letter. An example of a T-chart contrasting reptiles and amphibians is shown in Figure 47–2.

REFERENCES

Brett, J. (1994). *The town mouse and the country mouse.* New York: Philomel.
Cauley, L. B. (1984). *The town mouse and the country mouse.* New York: Putnam.

Word Sorts

● literature focus units	● preK	● individual
● literature circles	● K–2	● pairs
○ reading-writing workshop	● 3–5	● small group
● thematic units	● 6–8	● whole class

Word sorts is a strategy for examining and categorizing words according to their meanings, sound-symbol correspondences, or spelling patterns (Bear, Invernizzi, Templeton, & Johnston, 1996; Schlagal & Schlagal, 1992). The purpose of word sorts is to help students focus on conceptual and phonological features of words and identify recurring patterns. For example, as students sort word cards with words such as *stopping, eating, hugging, running,* and *raining,* they discover the rule for doubling the final consonant in short-vowel words before adding an inflectional ending.

Students sort a group of words, objects, or pictures according to the following:

- conceptual relationships, such as words related to different characters in a story
- rhyming words, such as words that rhyme with *ball, cat, car,* and *rake*
- consonant sounds, such as pictures and objects of words beginning with *r* or *l*
- sound-symbol relationships, such as words in which the final *y* sounds like long *i* (*cry*) and words in which the final *y* sounds like long *e* (*baby*)
- spelling patterns and rules, such as long *e* words with various spelling patterns (*sea, greet, be, Pete*)
- number of syllables, such as *pig, happy, afternoon,* and *television*
- root words and affixes
- homonyms

Many of the words chosen for word sorts should come from books students are reading or across-the-curriculum thematic units. Figure 48–1 shows a first-grade word sort using words from Nancy Shaw's *Sheep in a Jeep* (1986), *Sheep on a Ship* (1989), and *Sheep in a Shop* (1991). Students sorted the words according to three rimes—*eep, ip,* and *op.*

STEP BY STEP

The steps in doing a word sort are:

1. *Choose a topic.* Teachers choose a language skill or content-area topic for the word sort and decide whether it will be an open or closed sort. In an open sort, students determine the categories themselves based on the words they are sorting. In a closed sort, teachers present the categories as they introduce the sorting activity.

2. *Compile a list of words.* Teachers compile a list of 6 to 20 words, depending on grade level, that exemplify particular categories, and write the words on small cards. Or, small objects or picture cards can be used.

3. *Introduce the sorting activity to a small group or to the class.* If it is a closed sort, teachers present the categories for the sort and have students sort word cards, picture cards, or small objects into these

 Students who are learning English benefit from opportunities to manipulate word cards when they do word sorts in small groups. Having the words to manipulate makes the activity more concrete, and students can add small pictures to the cards to aid in identifying the words. Also, their classmates assist in pronouncing words and explaining the meanings of words.

FIGURE 48–1 A First-Grade Class's Word Sort Using Words From Nancy Shaw's "Sheep" Books

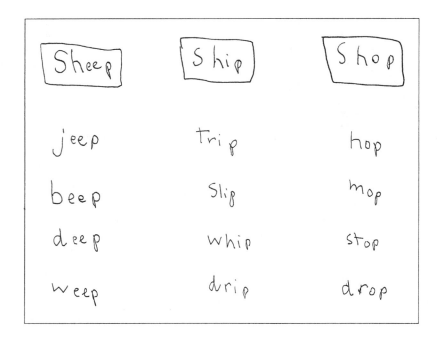

categories. If it is an open sort, students identify the words, pictures, or objects and look for possible categories. Students arrange and rearrange the cards or objects into various categories until they are satisfied with the sorting. Then they add category labels.

4. *Make a permanent record.* Students make a permanent record of their sort. They glue the word or picture cards onto a large sheet of construction paper or poster board. Or, students write the words or draw pictures on sheets of paper, as shown in Figure 48–1.

5. *Share word sorts.* Students share their word sorts with classmates, emphasizing the categories they used for them.

APPLICATIONS AND EXAMPLES

Students sort small objects and pictures as well as word cards. For example, to develop phonemic awareness, young children sort objects according to rhyming patterns (e.g., *cat, hat, bat,* and *mat*) or by beginning sound (e.g., *lion, letter, lollipop, lemon*). They can also sort pictures of plants according to the type of plant (e.g., trees, flowers, fruits, vegetables), or sort gods and goddesses according to ancient civilization (e.g., ancient Egypt, ancient Greece, ancient Rome).

Fourth- and fifth-grade English learners studying transportation sorted small plastic models and pictures of land, water, and air transportation and then created the word sort shown in Figure 48–2.

Land	Water	Air
car	ship	jet
truck	rowboat	helicopter
bicycle	sailboat	hot air balloon
horse	motorboat	airplane
taxi cab	barge	spaceship
elevator	submarine	
train	tanker	
subway		
bus		

FIGURE 48–2   EL Students' Transportation Word Sort

REFERENCES

Bear, D. R., Invernizzi, M., Templeton, S., & Johnston, F. (1996). *Words their way: Word study for phonics, vocabulary, and spelling instruction.* Upper Saddle River, NJ: Merrill/Prentice Hall.

Schlagal, R. C., & Schlagal, J. H. (1992). The integral character of spelling: Teaching strategies for multiple purposes. *Language Arts, 69,* 418–424.

Shaw, N. (1986). *Sheep in a jeep.* Boston: Houghton Mifflin.

Shaw, N. (1989). *Sheep on a ship.* Boston: Houghton Mifflin.

Shaw, N. (1991). *Sheep in a shop.* Boston: Houghton Mifflin.

Word Walls

- ● literature focus units
- ○ literature circles
- ○ reading-writing workshop
- ● thematic units

- ● preK
- ● K–2
- ● 3–5
- ● 6–8

- ○ individual
- ○ pairs
- ○ small group
- ● whole class

Word walls are large sheets of butcher paper on which students and the teacher write interesting, confusing, and important words from stories, informational books, and textbooks they are reading (Tompkins, 2003). Students refer to the words on the word wall for writing activities and for word-study activities. A fourth-grade class's alphabetized word wall for *Sarah, Plain and Tall* (MacLachlan, 1983) is shown in Figure 49–1.

Other word walls can be developed for social studies and science thematic units. A kindergarten or first-grade word wall on plants might include these key words: *seeds, flowers, stem, trees, cactus, roots, sunshine, water, soil, leaves,* and *grow.* Teachers prepare separate word walls for different curricular areas so that students will categorize the words more easily. If words related to a literature focus unit on *Sarah, Plain and Tall* and words related to a thematic unit on machines are mixed together, for example, students may become confused.

STEP BY STEP

The steps in using a word wall are:

1. *Prepare the word wall.* Teachers hang a long sheet of butcher paper on a blank wall in the classroom, divide it into 12 to 16 boxes, and label with letters of the alphabet.

2. *Introduce the word wall.* Teachers introduce the word wall and write several key words on it during preparing activities before reading.

3. *Add words to the word wall.* After reading a picture book or after reading each chapter of a chapter book, students suggest other "important" words for the word wall. Students and the teacher write the words on the butcher paper, making sure to write large enough so that most students can see the word. If a word is misspelled, it should be corrected because students will be reading and using the word in various activities. Sometimes the teacher adds a small picture or writes a synonym for a difficult word, puts a box around the root word, or writes the plural form or other related words nearby.

 Word walls are a valuable resource for English learners, especially when small illustrations are added next to each word. Students practice reading the words and using them in sentences they are speaking and writing. They can also select the most important words to write and illustrate on a personal word wall.

4. *Use the word wall for exploring activities.* Students use the words for a variety of activities, and teachers expect them to spell the words correctly. During literature focus units, students refer to the word wall when they are making words, writing in reading logs, doing word sorts, or working on projects. During thematic units, students use the word wall in similar ways.

5. *Write the words on word cards.* Teachers transfer the words from the word wall to word cards at the end of the literature focus unit or thematic unit. They can write the words on index cards, sentence strips, or small sheets of decorated paper that correspond to the topic of the unit. They punch holes in one corner of the cards and use metal rings or yarn to make a booklet. They place the word booklets in the writing center for students to refer to as needed.

A	B	C	D
Anna	biscuits	coarse	dough
ayuh	bonnet	conch shell	dunes
	blue flax	Caleb	
		cruel	
		crowding	
		chores	
		collapsed	
		carpenter	
		colored pencils	
EF	**G**	**HI**	**JK**
feisty	gophers	hearthstones	
eagerly		Indian paintbrush	
fogbound		hollow	
energetic		homely	
		housekeeper	
		holler	
		horrid	
		harshly	
LM	**NO**	**PQ**	**RS**
mild mannered	offshore	Papa	stalls
longing	oyster	paddock	roamer
mica	nip	patches	rascal
		pesky	shovel
		preacher	suspenders
		prairie	slab
		pitchfork	shuffling
			smoothing
			Sarah
			slippery
			squall
T	**UV**	**W**	**XYZ**
troublesome		wretched	
treaded water		woodchuck	
tumbleweed		wooly ragwort	
		wild-eyed	
		windbreak	
		whooped	
		widened	

FIGURE 49–1   A word wall for *Sarah, Plain and Tall*

AB	C	D	EF
Asher	Ceremony of Twelves	dwelling	Elevens
bicycles	comfort object	dark brown	family unit
assignment	climate control	designated areas	Fiona
aptitude	commerce	disregarded rules	elders
birth mothers	consciousness	destination	emotional
apprehensive	counsel		flee
burdensome	Christmas lights		escape
anguished	chute		Elsewhere
	courage		efficient
			exquisite
			fugitives
G	H	IJ	KL
Gabriel	horror	Jonas	Lily
Giver	hearing-beyond	inadequate	landscape
glumly		intrigued	lied
		inconvenient	limp
		journey	
M	NO	PQR	S
memory	Nurturer	release	spouses
	name tag	puberty	stirrings
	nurture	prestige	sameness
	newchild	precision	shade
	numb	Receiver	syringe
		pale	scold
		red apple	survive
		regret	shuddering
		plea	sarcastic
		pills	successor
		puncture	snowflake
		realization	squirm
			shocked
			sensation
			seeing-beyond
T	UV	WX	YZ
tunic	undertaking	winced	
transit	vigilant	wisp	
transgressions			
training			
terrible pain			
tidy			

FIGURE 49–2   An Eighth Grader's Word Wall for *The Giver*

FIGURE 49–3 The "A" Page From a First-Grade Word Wall of High-Frequency Words

APPLICATIONS AND EXAMPLES

For kindergartners and other emergent readers, teachers often write key words on small cards and place them in a pocket chart instead of writing the words on a word wall. When the words are written on cards, students can match the words to objects and pictures and use them for other activities. For a literature focus unit on *Rosie's Walk* (Hutchins, 1968), for example, key words might include *Rosie, hen, fox, farm, rake, bees, wagon, mill,* and *flour.*

Older students make individual word walls on sheets of paper or file folders divided in boxes and labeled with letters of the alphabet. As they read a novel or study a social studies or science unit, the students add words to complete their word walls. Figure 49–2 shows an eighth grader's word wall with nearly 100 words from *The Giver* (Lowry, 1993).

A second type of word wall for high-frequency words is used in primary-grade classrooms. Teachers hang large sheets of construction paper, one for each letter of the alphabet, on a wall of the classroom, and then post high-frequency words such as *the, is, are, you, what,* and *to* as they are introduced (Cunningham, 1995). Figure 49–3 shows a sheet of "A" words developed in a first-grade classroom. Students also added small picture cards with other interesting words. This word wall remains on display, and additional words are added throughout the year. In kindergarten classrooms, teachers begin the school year by having students write their names on the wall chart and add common environmental print, such as K-Mart and McDonald's. Later in the year, they add words such as *I, love, the, you, Mom, Dad, good,* and other words that students want to be able to read and write.

REFERENCES

Cunningham, P. M. (1995). *Phonics they use: Words for reading and writing* (2nd ed.). New York: HarperCollins.

Hutchins, P. (1968). *Rosie's walk.* New York: Macmillan.

Lowry, L. (1993). *The giver.* Boston: Houghton Mifflin.

MacLachlan, P. (1983). *Sarah, plain and tall.* New York: Harper & Row.

Tompkins, G. E. (2003). *Literacy for the 21st century* (3rd ed.). Upper Saddle River, NJ: Merrill/Prentice Hall.

50 Writing Groups

- ● literature focus units
- ○ literature circles
- ● reading-writing workshop
- ● thematic units

- ○ preK
- ● K–2
- ● 3–5
- ● 6–8

- ○ individual
- ○ pairs
- ● small group
- ○ whole class

During the revising stage of the writing process, students meet in writing groups to share their rough drafts and get feedback on how well they are communicating (Tompkins, 2004). Revising is probably the most difficult part of the writing process because it is difficult for students to stand back and evaluate their writing objectively in order to make changes so that their writing communicates more effectively. As students participate in writing groups, they learn how to work together and to provide useful feedback to classmates.

STEP BY STEP

The steps in conducting a writing group are:

1. *Read drafts aloud.* Students take turns reading their rough drafts aloud to the group. Everyone listens politely, thinking about compliments and suggestions they will make after the writer finishes reading. Only the writer looks at the composition because when classmates and the teacher look at it, they quickly notice and comment on mechanical errors, even though the emphasis during revising is on content. Listening to the writing read aloud keeps the focus on content.

2. *Offer compliments.* After listening to the rough draft read aloud, classmates in the writing group tell the writer what they liked about the composition. These positive comments should be specific, focusing on strengths, rather than the often-heard "I liked it" or "It was good"; even though these are positive comments, they do not provide effective feedback. Possible topics for students to comment on are:

leads	word choice	voice
dialogue	golden sentences	rhyme
endings	character development	sequence
description	point of view	flashbacks
innovations	literary opposites	alliterations

   When teachers introduce revision, they should model appropriate responses because students may not know how to offer specific and meaningful comments. Teachers and students can brainstorm a list of appropriate comments and post it in the classroom for students to refer to. Possible comments are:

   I like the part where . . .

   I'd like to know more about . . .

   I like the way you described . . .

   Your writing made me feel . . .

   I like the order you used in your writing because . . .

3. *Ask clarifying questions.* After a round of positive comments, writers ask for assistance with trouble spots they identified earlier when rereading their writing, or they may ask questions that

reflect more general concerns about how well they are communicating. Admitting the need for help from classmates is a major step in learning to revise. Possible questions to classmates are:

What do you want to know more about?

Is there a part that I should throw away?

What details can I add?

What do you think is the best part of my writing?

Are there some words I need to change?

4. *Offer other revision suggestions.* Members of the writing group ask questions about things that were unclear to them and make suggestions about how to revise the composition. Almost any writer resists constructive criticism, and it is especially difficult for elementary students to appreciate suggestions. It is important to teach students what kinds of comments and suggestions are acceptable so that they will word what they say in helpful rather than hurtful ways. Possible comments and suggestions that students can offer are:

I got confused in the part about . . .

Do you need a closing?

Could you add more about . . .

I wonder if your paragraphs are in the right order . . .

Could you combine some sentences?

5. *Repeat the process.* Members of the writing group repeat the process so that all students can share their rough drafts. The first four steps are repeated for each student's composition. This is the appropriate time for teachers to provide input as well.

6. *Make plans for revision.* At the end of the writing group session, students each make a commitment to revise their writing based on the comments and suggestions of the group members. The final decisions on what to revise always rest with the writers themselves, but with the understanding that their rough drafts are not perfect comes the realization that some revision will be necessary. When students verbalize their planned revisions, they are more likely to complete the revision stage. Some students also make notes for themselves about their revision plans. After the group disbands, students make the revisions.

APPLICATIONS AND EXAMPLES

Students often meet with the same writing group throughout the school year, or students can form groups when they are ready to get feedback about their rough drafts. When students are working together on a writing project, such as writing a sequel after reading a book during a literature focus unit or writing reports on desert plants and animals as part of a thematic unit on the desert, many students will be ready to meet in writing groups at approximately the same time, so they can meet in groups according to established groups in the classroom. In contrast, during writing workshop, students work on writing projects at their own speed, and students need to meet in writing groups at different times. Many teachers have students sign up on the chalkboard; this way, whenever four or five students are ready, they form a group. Both established and spontaneously formed groups can be effective. What matters most is that students get feedback about their writing when they need it.

REFERENCE

Tompkins, G. E. (2004). *Teaching writing: Balancing process and product* (4th ed.). Upper Saddle River, NJ: Merrill/Prentice Hall.